OZ

A HITCHHIKER'S

AUSTRALIAN

ANTHOLOGY

ALSO BY JONATHAN NICHOLAS

Hospital Beat
Kibbutz Virgin
The Tragic Romance of Africa

JONATHAN NICHOLAS

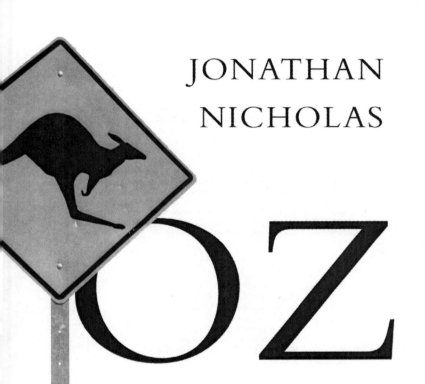

OZ

A HITCHHIKER'S AUSTRALIAN ANTHOLOGY

Matador
9 Priory Business Park,
Wistow Road, Kibworth Beauchamp,
Leicestershire. LE8 0RX
Tel: (+44) 116 279 2299
Fax: (+44) 116 279 2277
Email: books@troubador.co.uk
Web: www.troubador.co.uk/matador

ISBN 978 1783064 809

British Library Cataloguing in Publication Data.
A catalogue record for this book is available from the British Library.

Typeset in StempelGaramond Roman by Troubador Publishing Ltd
Printed and bound in the UK by TJ International, Padstow, Cornwall

Matador is an imprint of Troubador Publishing Ltd

To Australia

This is a true story

Australia's major road network

I love a sunburnt country,
A land of sweeping plains,
Of ragged mountain ranges,
Of droughts and flooding rains.
I love her far horizons,
I love her jewel-sea,
Her beauty and her terror –
The wide brown land for me!

CONTENTS

PREFACE

I spent a very odd year in Australia when I was twenty-two years old. It was a very eventful, challenging, dangerous and wonderful year and one that, as you will see, was totally unforgettable. I was young, adventurous and very determined, but at times I was also unbelievably stupid and naïve. Quite often I involved myself in things which perhaps I should be too embarrassed or ashamed to reveal and which some people have told me should not be included in this book, but I don't regret a single moment of it as it all meshed together to create my crazy year in that wonderful country.

I lived the life of a penniless vagrant for some of the time and for a while I also drove around in my own company car, such was the way my life in Oz took some radical changes of fortune. I had already been away from home for almost two years when I left the easy and comfortable life on Kibbutz Be'eri in Israel for a risky and uncertain existence in Australia. So what happened to me when I crossed the world and arrived down under?

After arriving in Sydney I lived underneath some stairs like Harry Potter in a strange house for weeks with a woman who sat knitting and smoking dope all night, every night. When I left there I started renting a room in a cockroach infested tenement close to the world famous Bondi beach. The house in Bondi was also occupied by some very unconventional people, who I tried my best to avoid while I spent many long carefree sunny afternoons body surfing and sleeping on the beach. In the evenings I worked in a very strange job selling acrylic paintings door to door. I moved north to sub-tropical Brisbane and rented a flat with a gay New Zealander whose brother was a cannabis dealer on the nearby Gold Coast. I then discovered what a 'bong' was and a 'mull bowl' and spent the next few months quite detached from reality as a result.

I didn't plan my trip very well because, during most of my

time in Australia, I was an illegal over-stayer on a six week tourist visa. I couldn't claim state benefits and I had no official work permit, and so I had to take any casual work I could find in order to survive. Quite often I had little or no money in my pockets and at the end of it all I weighed less than ten stone (or 140 pounds) having lost almost a quarter of my body weight. In fact, within days of my arrival in Australia I remember walking across Sydney Harbour Bridge with empty pockets and an even emptier stomach. How on earth did I manage to survive for a further twelve months?

As usual I kept detailed diaries of my adventures, writing regularly of the events, the people, the sights, and more importantly some of my inner-most thoughts of the time. The undoubted highlight of this astonishing experience and perhaps the main reason for my visit was my wonderful hitchhiking adventure across the vast sunburnt continent. From Brisbane up to Townsville, across Queensland to Mount Isa, up to Darwin in the tropical Northern Territory, through the desert wilderness to Alice Springs, across the Woomera Prohibited Area to Adelaide, then to Melbourne, on to Sydney, and back up to Brisbane. I crossed Australia travelling more than 6,000 miles (10,000 kilometres) using nothing more than my thumb and some quiet determination.

At some point during my year there I fell hopelessly in love with Australia. Maybe it happened in the back of the Holden Ute at midnight when looking up at the stars as I crossed the spectacular emptiness of central Queensland. It could have been during my lift with Rod and Ritchie from Darwin to Katherine while we smoked Sinsemilla, drank ice-cold beer and listened to *The Rolling Stones*. I think it was probably when I woke up in my little tent at Julia Creek and saw remote central Queensland in daylight for the first time. One thing is for certain; when I eventually left Australia this fabulous continent had left a permanent impression and changed me forever.

Jonathan Nicholas
March 2014

THE NEGEV DESERT, ISRAEL

Leaving paradise

The figure on the grassy slope half-a-mile away vanished. I watched as it reappeared, reaching the top of the crest on what would probably still be soft and stodgy earth from recent rains. The Negev Desert was like that in winter. One minute it was dusty-dry and in the next moment huge blue-black cumulus clouds would gather and produce flash floods that in an instant would turn the many dry *wadis* into deep, fast-flowing torrents. Between December and February this could happen at any time, and was usually followed by spectacular displays of thrusting new growth from the ubiquitous red poppies and daisies that sprang up in patches all across the land.

I watched as the figure joined the path which ran around the field and then disappeared again. But then the top of the person's head was visible, bobbing along like a football drifting slowly down a stream. Then it rose up to full height, standing rigid, legs apart, looking in my direction, as if scrutinizing me from afar. I was annoyed that I couldn't see who it was or communicate with them. I felt inside my coat pocket for my pen knife and opened out the blade. Looking up at the sky I aimed it towards the sun and tried signalling to the figure. It then descended the slope again and disappeared into the myriad of wet, sandy *wadis*.

It was probably Paul. I'd told him where I'd be before I left. We'd been picking oranges together all morning in the *pardes* (Hebrew word for 'paradise' and where the oranges grow) and we often spent time wandering about in the desert. Paul was keen on photography and had taken hundreds of pictures in and around the kibbutz. I just loved being alone sometimes, and the emptiness of the Negev Desert was the ideal place to enjoy some quiet solitude, to sit and contemplate, or just spend some time writing in my diary.

I wondered about the figure again. I hoped it would be Paul but it could also have been Sean. I didn't want to see Sean just then. There were certain times when Sean's humour and sheer presence was a tonic for me, but not at that moment. We'd talked, laughed and joked the night before with the girls, Jane and Anika, in Sean's room, the four of us starting and finishing off a bottle of Israeli gin between us. The cheap booze seemed to have no effect on us, but I could sense some antagonism from the start and a mounting atmosphere of paranoia lurking around the dark corners of the shabby, little room. I felt incredibly uncomfortable. I cracked what I knew to be terrible jokes in a hopeless effort to rescue the atmosphere. Maybe it was all in my own head?

I'd been back at kibbutz Be'eri for six months and I was becoming impatient with the beautiful inertia of my life in paradise. Dare I admit that I was getting a little bored with it? It was my second six months at Be'eri and my third six month stint on a kibbutz if you included kibbutz Dafna in the north a couple of years before. Was it possible to have enough of paradise? Or even to have too much of a good thing?

I felt around in my pocket and opened a new pack of Nelson cigarettes, screwing up the crisp cellophane and tossing it carelessly in front of me. I lit one and drew in the smoke, blowing it back out across the desert. A horse appeared in the middle of a huge rolling field to my left. The rider was wearing a bright yellow shirt or was it a woollen jumper? It was still too far away to see who it was, or even whether it was a man or a woman, riding now back up the slope, and then halting on the crest, glancing around, before riding away into the distance. The desert *wadis* outside the kibbutz looked particularly beautiful that afternoon, and there was always a peculiar illusion of distance, as though the observer was looking across the far grander Judean hills but on a much smaller scale.

I'd been sitting out there all alone on one previous occasion when Tomer had come galloping up, riding a huge, brown beast of a thing which looked utterly magnificent against the desert scenery. I happened to mention that I couldn't remember the last time I'd been on a horse, so Tomer insisted I climb aboard, and then we walked through some nearby trees and back onto the road, calmly and gently, as though we were on Skegness pleasure beach. But it wasn't Tomer this time, and I watched as the horse walked the rider slowly into the trees around the distant Anzac Memorial and the old kibbutz before disappearing from view completely.

I then heard a series of dull thuds in the earth, not as heavy as a horse but more like a person running, behind the bottom end of the same slope I was sitting on. If it was Paul heading towards me, there was a good chance he may try sneaking up on me but then the figure reappeared again somewhere else. It was standing perfectly still against the horizon this time, fully erect, away to the east. I reached in my rucksack for a Goldstar beer and another cigarette. I didn't take my eyes off the stranger in the near distance. *Who the hell was it?* I thought to myself. Maybe it wasn't Paul? No-one appeared up the slope, so what were the noises in the earth I'd heard earlier? I blew my cigarette smoke out in a series of perfectly formed smoke rings which were gently grabbed by a passing breeze and carried along slowly, growing fainter as they drifted away and eventually vanished.

After sitting there for a while, busily daydreaming, I shivered very slightly; the wind was just beginning to cool as the sun was now lower, ever closer to the horizon beyond the incredible festering mess that was Gaza city five miles away. I thought of all the occasions I'd hitchhiked to and from Gaza and even crawled under the fence past the Israeli checkpoints to get to the sea. My Danish friend, Henrik, and I used to sit overlooking the Mediterranean Sea in a tumble-down café listening to the elderly Palestinian proprietor tell us wistfully of the better days.

I'd hitchhiked up to Tel Aviv on numerous occasions and I'd recently spent a few days in the north with Paul, hitchhiking around Kiryat Shmona in the Upper Galilee. We hitchhiked everywhere and we were quite accomplished at it. It was a very good form of transport in Israel: fast, efficient, and obviously very cheap.

I glanced around instinctively for firewood for later on, just in case. I couldn't sit there alone in the dark though, could I? I was listening to the exquisite silence of the desert when the figure reappeared again. I waved, calmly, slowly, and then it turned and began walking towards me. The slim frame inside the green combat jacket, faded blue jeans, camera hanging around the neck, I knew then that it was indeed Paul.

He sat beside me on the yellow desert earth, his long thin fingers fiddling with his Pentax camera. I handed him a small bottle of Goldstar and we sat together drinking and smoking for a while, gazing out across the empty Negev. Gradually as it grew darker, lights began to appear in Gaza, twinkling delicately in the distance just like the stars above us. We had to get back to the kibbutz for dinner.

As we walked we discussed my imminent departure from paradise. It was the end of an era for me and I was finally moving on. It was to be the last time I'd live and work on a kibbutz (despite the recent arrival of a group of tall, slim, Finnish girls all with white-blonde, shoulder-length hair) but Australia was waiting for me, and I thought I was ready for it.

ATHENS AIRPORT, GREECE

A QANTAS of solace

I sat near the QANTAS desk in Athens airport waiting to check in. As I did so, I observed a clumsy group of package holidaymakers huddled together, reluctant to converse with one another but clinging to each other like limpets lest they had to make conversation with any of the locals. When one of them spoke to someone who clearly did not understand or speak English they raised their voices and waved their arms around wildly as though talking to a deaf idiot. Every time I saw this I couldn't decide whether to laugh or cry. They were probably British, because we are very good at assuming the whole world has to speak to us in English. What possessed them to even want to return to the damp and dreary British Isles anyway? The place was a mess. Or was it the possibility they were a reminder to me of why I was escaping, and of the year I'd spent working in a bank in Grantham, once voted *the* most boring town in England? I'd failed in the bank, so were they a reminder of my failure?

I'd schemed, planned, joked and dreamed so many times of 'a great adventure', at first probably just idle boasts to friends, or some unrealistic and outrageous fantasy. But there I was, in Athens airport awaiting a flight to the other side of the world, and my British friends were – presumably – still in England. I then counted in my head how many really good friends I'd made in the previous few years. A good friend I defined as someone you could call on for help, comfort, and honesty, both in the good times and the bad, all the qualities which make someone special and elevate them above the ambiguous, lesser title of 'acquaintance'. It seemed I didn't have that many.

I looked at the clock on the wall. I was anxious to get airborne but there was still a three hour wait before I was bound for Bangkok and then Sydney. I decided that one day I'd like to visit Japan. A dozen Nippon beauties with petite figures and long, straight, black hair glided past me, dragging their bags behind them. They had endless smiles across their gorgeous round faces, they seemed hugely dignified and I immediately fell in love with every single one of them. But then in another moment they had passed me and were gone. In a few more minutes they could be on their way home and in twelve hours they might be on the other side of the world. Nothing lasts forever. Why couldn't time stand still? Why couldn't we capture and save a special moment in our lives and preserve it like a pickled onion in a jar, to be reopened and savoured at our leisure?

I began to ponder the life I had just left behind on the kibbutz, and the friends I'd left: Sean, Jane, Anika, Paul and Jacko. With each one of them I was a slightly different person, but aren't we all like that with our friends? They say you should never put all your friends together in one room, they just wouldn't get on. I needed some new friendships, because the ones I already had seemed to be wearing a little thin, like the soles of an aging pair of dearly loved slippers. One of the wonders of travel is meeting new people, most of whom pass us by without leaving any lingering impression. But there are the others, few in number in anyone's life, who we really miss. We miss them badly, painfully, like a burning, aching wound eating away at us, but then this is the price to be paid for the pure joy of meeting them again later. It's better than any drug – the intimacy of good friends whether they are male or female, sexual or not. Something unspoken is shared, some invisible and inexplicable attraction that lasts across all time and space.

Check-in opened and I put my one small rucksack onto the scales. It was weighed and tagged and then slung quite carelessly through some black plastic strips and was gone. I wanted to ask them to be particularly careful with it, because that insignificant little bag contained my whole world. It was all I had, just a thin nylon sleeping bag, a change of clothing, a few papers, some pens and a sketch book. I always kept my diary and a paperback book with me, on my person. I never knew when I might need to write, and so I didn't ever want to leave myself vulnerable with nothing to write in or on. My diary was everything to me.

I drank a couple of beers in the bar and sat reading my book. I felt like a true jetsetter, about to board a plane for the other side of the world. I'd never been to Australia before. It was such a long way from Europe, and I was impressed by its sheer distance from everywhere else. On reflection I wonder now if I was more stupid than I was naïve, thinking that I could travel to a place like Australia and make a success of my visit, let alone survive it intact. It was a huge place and I knew absolutely nothing about it.

As I sat observing my fellow passengers I thought about how people suddenly looked different, or was it just that I felt different from them? We are all conditioned by the place we come from, by our own culture and ethnicity. I could tell many of these people might be Australian. But this conditioning can dissolve away over time, until eventually people can become independent of their own cultural way of thinking. This was part of the broadening of the mind through travel. I'd already been away from England for almost two years and was beginning to enjoy feeling very slightly stateless and dispossessed.

I made the mistake of keeping my penknife in my pocket and not in my checked baggage, so it was confiscated by security. I'd have to buy another from somewhere when I arrived in Australia. I boarded the Boeing 747 with great anticipation and, as usual, I was very excited when the huge lumbering aircraft roared down the runway, hauling itself slowly into the air like a beautiful but very heavy swan rising majestically from a lake.

As soon as we achieved level flight some lovely cooking smells filled the cabin, and after a particularly tasty QANTAS meal of hot roast chicken and vegetables followed by several cups of sweet tea I adjusted my seat back a little to enjoy the flight. I was happy and relieved to be on my way at last, even though I had no idea what was going to happen to me. I closed my eyes and relaxed, it wasn't long before I fell asleep.

SYDNEY, AUSTRALIA

"You wanna smoke?"

I woke up hours later when some fellow passengers on the right side of the cabin began lifting the shades from over their windows. Brilliant sunshine began streaming in across the aircraft cabin like wide shafts of bright light penetrating a gloomy church. It was almost too bright to look at and everyone then began to stir awake, just as yet more wonderful cooking smells drifted in from the galley. Blankets were folded up and seats were lifted straight as a tasty breakfast was served by fussy and attentive cabin crew. Not long afterwards the plane descended bumpily through some dense clouds and landed quite heavily on a water-logged runway in tropical Bangkok. It was daylight and very bright, despite the heavy rain.

I wandered around the overcrowded and claustrophobic transit lounge for half an hour feeling particularly crumpled and sweaty before the flight was recalled for boarding. Several hours later after more food and sleep the aircraft landed on Australian soil in Melbourne to pick up and unload goods and passengers before taking off yet again. Finally it reached its ultimate destination, Sydney, Australia's biggest city, and the most common starting point for visitors to the country.

Huge colour photographs of famous Australian landmarks lined the corridors into the arrivals hall; the Opera House, the Harbour Bridge, Ayer's Rock, and wonderful images of scantily clad women in crystal clear water swimming around the Great Barrier Reef. One particular photograph grabbed my attention more than all the others as I walked by it, so much so that I had to stop dead still for a moment just to gaze at it. It was a wide-angle shot of absolutely nothing. That is, it was an amazing photograph of the outback, showing the deep red earth and barren rocks stretching away as far as the eye could see, topped with a deeply blue cloudless sky. To me this was the real Australia, and I made a mental note that whatever happened I must see at least some of this.

I collected my rucksack from the carousel and joined the long queues that snaked their way to the customs desks, passing frequent warning signs against importing fruit, vegetables, nuts and other plant and animal life. My passport was checked by a smiling immigration officer and then I was free to enter the country.

A nervous phone call and an apprehensive taxi ride to an address followed. Things didn't work out quite as planned and I found myself taking up residence under a stranger's stairs in an old townhouse in the inner city suburb of Darlinghurst. My complete lack of planning and preparation became obvious because I didn't know what to do with myself. In addition to this I found the first few days in the country were spent trying to adjust physically and mentally to an opposite time zone. I was very drowsy in the evenings and wide awake in the early mornings. I fought it as best I could but it still took several days to overcome. I was staying in the house of a friend of a friend who I didn't know. I didn't even know how long I could stay, but I knew I wasn't much of a burden because I didn't eat any of their food and only took up a small amount of space underneath the open-plan staircase on the ground floor close to the kitchen door. I was to become quite accustomed to sleeping on the floor.

I drifted quite absentmindedly into spending my first few days in Australia exploring Sydney. The SCG (the Sydney Cricket Ground) was nearby so I took a look at that first. It was hallowed ground and I'd seen it so often on the television, usually when the England cricket team were getting soundly thrashed by the Aussies. Then I ventured further and wandered down through the city to Circular Quay, the Opera House and the Harbour Bridge. I found it very strange and extremely exciting to see these iconic buildings so close up. I touched the Opera House reverently with the palm of my right hand and saw that the huge shell-like roof structures were actually made up of thousands of shiny, white tiles about six inches across, like a huge mosaic. In this respect it reminded me a little of the fabulous Dome of the Rock mosque on Temple Mount in Jerusalem, the outside walls of which are decorated with millions of tiny and beautifully coloured mosaic pieces. The bridge was much bigger than I had imagined, and it carried a wide and very busy roadway across it. I couldn't help but notice some of the huge steel girders that I could see had 'Made in England' imprinted on them. In fact if you live in England you can see a smaller version of the same bridge in Newcastle; the Tyne Bridge is an exact copy and both bridges were built at roughly the same time in the late 1920s.

Circular Quay is a railway station and also the main quay for all the ferry boats which crisscross their way around the harbour from north to south, under the bridge to Darling Harbour and in the opposite direction past Cremorne Point and Watson's Bay to Manly. These ferries all seemed reasonably priced, prompt and very frequent. My initial thoughts were that Sydney was an extremely exciting place, lively and interesting, with plenty to see, and I hadn't visited any of the wonderful beaches yet. I didn't think at that time to look for a job, not straight away, perhaps I should have done. Instead I returned every night to the house in Darlinghurst to sleep in my little space under the stairs.

Because I stayed out of the house for most of the day until the late evening I didn't really get to know anyone else living there except for one person, a thin woman in her mid-thirties who had a pale, almost anaemic complexion and curly, shoulder-length yellow hair. I saw her drift silently past me like a ghost several times very late during the first few nights I was there when she went into the kitchen to make a cup of tea. I could see she was boiling a kettle and stirring a cup and if I wasn't asleep I would speak to her briefly every time she passed. Eventually on my third night she paused for a moment and stood with her cup of tea looking down at me on the floor. Looking quite blankly at me she said:

"You wanna smoke?" to which I replied politely and with some surprise:

"Sure, why not?" as I began to shed my cocoon-like sleeping bag and stand up. I thought that at the very least I shouldn't be rude. I also felt quite alone and more than a little sorry for myself. What had I got to lose? I could do with some company and perhaps she could too. So I followed the woman into her room and as I walked in I could see the air inside was thick with a dense fog of cannabis and tobacco smoke. There was no light in the room save for a bright angle-poise lamp positioned above a chair in the middle where she obviously dwelt, permanently.

She sat down and immediately rolled a very long cannabis joint and then lit it with a match. For a while it just hung from her lips, dangling quite precariously and virtually immobile like an elongated Woodbine. She took the odd pull on it every now and again, leaving it untouched by her hands because surprisingly they were fully occupied with her knitting. I didn't think anybody knitted anymore. I sat on the floor next to her like an obedient puppy and after a while she passed the joint down to me and I took a long drag on it. It was hot, dry, and very strong.

I thought I might stay just for a few minutes but I actually stayed watching television with her for several hours, though I'm not sure exactly how long, before I thanked her and crawled back under the stairs and into my sleeping bag. I lay on my back for a while trying to count the steps above me before I drifted off to sleep in a whirling haze of cannabis intoxication.

I woke up the next morning feeling surprisingly fit and well, considering. From then on, at the end of every day I stayed up very late into the night with this woman, whose name I didn't know and who hardly ever spoke to me. She just sat in her chair avidly knitting and continually smoking very strong cannabis mixed with tobacco from my Camel cigarettes.

She developed a taste for the Israeli Nelson filter cigarettes too which I'd brought with me and she liked to use the milder tobacco in these to mix with the cannabis. Very soon they were all gone. The only thing she ever did seem to say to me frequently was: "Wanna smoke?" as she passed me the joints she'd rolled one after the other. The ends of her knitting needles made tiny metallic click-clack noises and the sight of her in that dreary little room bent over on her chair shrouded in a fog of smoke reminded me of my maternal grandmother who also used to sit smoking and knitting for hours whenever we visited her. I doubt she was chain smoking cannabis though.

On one particular late night smoking session with the knitting woman, we watched a movie with Derek Jacobi playing Hitler, on her small black and white television. The more I smoked the better the film became, and halfway through I noticed Hitler began wearing some bright green uniforms and long dark blue overcoats. How could a black and white television produce such vivid colours? It was all very strange, along with the fact that I never ever saw my knitting friend during the daylight hours. Though I was absent from the house for long periods of time she was never around when I was there and the door to her room was always firmly shut at all times before midnight. I also wondered how she could possibly concentrate on her knitting when she was so completely bombed off her tits all the time.

In the cool, clear straightness of morning each day I began to wonder what I was doing there, living under a stranger's stairs. My initial desire to socialise with the knitting woman for some company was now just a regular excuse to get smashed every night and I was beginning to lose touch. I was woken up each morning only a few hours after I'd gone to sleep by some people coming and going into the kitchen, presumably eating breakfast before going to work. Sometimes I'd only just drifted off to sleep as the sun was coming up, and when I was lying down my legs were stretched out full length inside the sleeping bag causing my feet to reach right into the kitchen doorway. I was aware of the occasional glancing contact with my feet sometimes, whether deliberate or not I would never know. I began to feel uncomfortable and I knew this arrangement couldn't last forever. I really wanted to leave, to move on, to live somewhere else, but I had very little money, not enough, and it was disappearing fast.

A week passed into another and then a third week arrived, drifting in slowly and largely unnoticed by me through a thick fog of cannabis smoke, some clattering of knitting needles and lots of late night TV movies. The smoking was making me lose focus and concentration and it would take others to eventually point out to me that I had to do something. There were snippets of overheard conversations in the house about me still being there, and how much longer was it going to be? I didn't know whose house it was, I still didn't know who the knitting woman was, or who anyone was for that matter, and in an increasingly rare moment of clarity and seriousness I suddenly realised that I had to get away. There must be a way of staying in Sydney and earning some money, if only I could find it.

Scouring the local newspaper one sunny afternoon I saw a job advertised selling artwork, with the promise of: 'Big bucks but no previous experience required!' It sounded too good to be true. It didn't come a moment too soon either, because earlier that same day I'd wandered dolefully across the Sydney Harbour Bridge on foot from a friend's place in Neutral Bay with frighteningly empty pockets, and not even enough to get back across the harbour by bus or ferry. I had no idea just how long the bridge was until I had to cross it on foot; it just seemed to stretch forever.

I had been keeping a few dollars in reserve for emergencies, and things that I really couldn't do without such as food. With barely enough money for the fare in the afternoon I caught a bus from Circular Quay to Bondi Junction in search of the wonderful job in the advert. I'd just spent my last few dollars, even my reserve food money, and I knew this could soon be it, the end.

If I didn't get something to earn money very soon I would be in some really deep shit.

BONDI JUNCTION

"A bloody Pom are you?"

At Bondi Junction I found the address in the advert for 'Décor Galleries' hidden unobtrusively amongst some shops on the busy main road. I pushed gently against a very austere looking brown door that was scuffed and cracked at the bottom, and walked up some steep, dark stairs into a large but sparsely furnished office. There were a few other people gathered around in the room, standing about in small groups or as nervous individuals. A thin man about my age appeared with a freshly lit cigarette in one hand, and who suddenly instructed all present in a very confident manner to sit facing him on the plastic chairs that lined the room. He then dragged a large blue folder towards him from a small adjoining office and opened it up.

Paintings were revealed, in garish colours and in relief, of typical Australian scenes. There was an old outback house with sloping corrugated iron roof set in parched yellow and red earth, a tropical waterfall in grey and blue shades called 'Blue Forest', a more distant farm house in flat Australian countryside with a windmill next to it, and an outback river scene called 'Blue Murray'. There were other scenes either in landscape or portrait, large and small. Each painting was on some kind of thin but quite heavy fibreboard, apparently called masonite, and came in two sizes, the standard A3 size and a few even larger ones.

I listened intently and understood that these were the products that were to be sold, but to whom and where? The standard size paintings were to be sold for a minimum of $35 and the larger ones for $45. These were the sums that were to be surrendered to the company after selling when you returned to the office. Anything above that amount was yours to keep, as commission. The thin man, Dave, began demonstrating to the audience how good the paintings were and how long it had taken him to paint each one, capturing the light here and there, the types of acrylic paint he used, and where he'd been sitting out in the bush to paint these fine works of Aussie art. There were dozens of these paintings all around the room in folders and stacked up neatly against the walls, all virtually identical. I thought this bloke had an incredible work rate and he must have been extremely busy with his paint brush.

I still hadn't a clue where and to whom these paintings were to be sold, as this still hadn't been fully explained. After twenty minutes of raving about the pictures they were packed away and the ensuing hush was broken by Dave and two other men handing out large heavy folders of paintings to anyone who wanted to give it a go. Several people just rose to their feet and fled, almost running for the door without saying anything to anyone, as though the fire alarm had just sounded. I was still seated and undecided when Dave thrust one of the folders at me.

"You wanna come with me? What's your name?"

"Jonathan," I replied rather sheepishly as though I was a young child just arrived for my first day at school. I was still pondering whether I should also quickly and quietly run for the exit. But now that I'd been spotted, and worse, actually spoken to directly, it might be a little more difficult to escape. I'd never sold anything before in my life and I had no idea whether I could do it.

I remained in my seat as though unable to stand, my mind clicking into the usual default mode of telling my body to do absolutely nothing. I remembered some of my flying training and the motto: 'Don't just do something – sit there!' This was the exact opposite of the instinctive urge when faced with a serious problem. It was meant to guard against dangerous over-reaction and panic when faced with a crisis in the cockpit, and it was sound advice. Allow some calm rational thought to prevail first before doing something in haste that you might regret, as in this case perhaps, running for the door. So I decided to go along with it, quite absentmindedly, drifting into it like so many other things I'd done before in my life, with little or no prior knowledge of what to expect.

I saw Dave pointing around the room at me and two others, and then he indicated for me to follow him out of the office and down the stairs, with a large folder of paintings. Out the back door this time, into a small car park, I sat in the cavernous rear of a huge dark brown car with another young man probably the same age as me. Another sat in the front seat before Dave jumped in and started the engine. The car was then driven away impatiently at such speed it was as though we'd just committed a bank robbery. I'd seen such driving only once before, as native French drivers negotiated their way anarchically around the Arc de Triumph in Paris during the weekday rush hour, in an almost total abandonment of any rules of the road.

The man in the front passenger seat spoke to Dave, who was smiling with a broad, cheesy grin across his thin, angular face while driving like a complete lunatic, weaving in and out of traffic, accelerating wildly then braking hard and changing lanes constantly. We three passengers sat in the car like nodding dogs with our heads bobbing around forwards and back then side to side. In fact the passenger in front of me looked from behind as though he was on an Olympic toboggan run his head was being thrown around so much. I'd never experienced anything like it, and it was clearly very dangerous, but I have to admit that I found it quite exciting too.

It was early evening and still light as the city streets flashed past while I sat in the back clutching the enormous folder, wondering what the hell I was doing. Where were we going? It still wasn't clear as to whom we were to attempt to sell the paintings. After more than half an hour of quite reckless yet strangely controlled driving as though Sydney's roads had become the Monaco race circuit, the car stopped abruptly at a wide and very open residential street corner. I have to admit that I'd been lazily gazing out the window by then, daydreaming of other things and other places. I'd almost forgotten why I was in the car when I was suddenly asked to get out.

"I'll pick you up back here in two hours, okay?" Dave said to me, with a very broad, fake smile and wide brown eyes.

"Yeah, sure," I replied, clumsily fumbling for the door handle. I climbed out with my heavy folder and stood on the corner as the car quickly sped away and was gone. I hadn't a clue where I was, other than it was clearly a reasonably well-to-do suburb of Sydney. I really hadn't been paying attention, and besides, I didn't know the city at all. I could have been in Parramatta or Pennant Hills, I wouldn't have a clue. The roads and houses all looked remarkably similar. I noticed in the inner suburbs there were older houses apparently made of wood but further out they were mostly made of brick and appeared to be more prosperous, though this wasn't always the case. They were all well-spaced and had huge wide front gardens and long driveways.

I tried to remember the name of the street and the time, because if I wasn't collected again I'd have absolutely no idea what to do. I crossed the road, the wide folder already uncomfortably heavy as it just fitted under my right arm. It was then that I realised to my dismay that I was obviously meant to sell the paintings door to door at the houses in front of me, so I took a deep breath and walked along the wide street to find somewhere to make a start.

I walked up the long steep driveway of the first house on the corner, pulled at the fly screen door, and propped it open with one leg. I could hear children inside the house, laughing and running around. I knocked on the door, balancing the folder on the ground against my other leg. I had to check my hands from visibly shaking, I was so nervous. My mouth was suddenly very dry and foolishly I realised too late that I hadn't a clue what I was going to say. I half hoped they wouldn't hear my knock so I could run away but then a man in a very loud shirt answered the door, pulling it open quickly with one hand, a can of beer in the other.

"Yes mate?" he said, firmly, with some obvious irritation

in his voice. I then rather stupidly said the first thing that leapt into my head:

"Well, I'm a Pom, and I thought you might like to look at these…" and before the folder was even opened the man replied in a booming voice:

"A bloody Pom are you?" He then turned and shouted behind him into the house in a very broad Aussie drawl: "Hey, there's a bloody Pom at the door here!" I smiled optimistically at this possible sign of hope, but then the man looked straight at me before saying calmly: "Sorry mate but you can *piss off*, right?" and slammed the door, laughing.

I stood on the doorstep for a few seconds, shocked and bewildered. This was clearly the wrong tack. I let the fly screen door spring shut and picked up the folder. After initially feeling terribly deflated by this man's comments I then felt a wave of anger sweep over me at the rude and unexpected rebuttal I'd just received. This was good in a way as it helped me to conquer my nerves. I needed to think fast though and change my tactics if I wasn't to return empty-handed, and more importantly, remain very hungry later. Perhaps I shouldn't have mentioned that I was an Englishman clearly straight off the plane? Maybe I should try to put on an Aussie accent?

I approached the next house with some positive determination and was all fired up for some decent sales talk I'd rehearsed in my head several times, but on this occasion and to my great disappointment no-one answered the door. I heaved the folder back up into my arms while trying to remain upbeat and walked up the neighbour's driveway. There were signs of life so I knocked loudly on the front door. When it was opened I fell straight into my new routine.

"Hi! How aaaaare ye? I got some 'o' me paindings heee, thought you mawt loyke te check 'em eeeeout?! I just done 'em in the bush eeeout back 'o' Bourke way!" I deliberately drew the vowel sounds out as long as I dare and avoided any eye contact at first, probably in case I felt my ruse might be discovered. The woman at the door – for I did notice the hem of a skirt at the open doorway – at least didn't slam it in my face immediately. She appeared to listen to me, probably in sympathy and sheer intrigue at hearing such an incredibly strange accent, before saying firmly but politely after several minutes:

"No thanks!" and then closed the door. It was an improvement on the first one, because she had actually listened for a while and didn't slam the door in my face. I tried each house in the street, and at every door I thoroughly embraced the local culture ever more by broadening my fake Aussie accent and remembering the 'rave' given earlier that night by Dave. I also repeated place names he had mentioned like Bourke and Wagga Wagga in the interior and dreamt up stories of extreme hardship while painting in the bush. I had no idea at that time just how prescient my stories of extreme hardship were.

I felt as though I was really struggling and began to think I'd never make any progress. As I continued trudging the clean, antiseptic streets of Sydney's middle class suburbia I imagined I was back in England, near my home town walking through the dense purple heather on the moors above the western fringes of Sheffield, the earthy damp peat smell filling my nostrils, and Mike Oldfield music bouncing around beautifully inside my head.

Several entire streets passed before I finally managed a bite. I was invited into the house of a man and woman in early middle-age whose lounge room I could see had a large and conspicuously blank wall which was just begging for a lovely picture. Without being prompted I opened my folder and held up a large Country Town painting and then the smaller version of the same thing. I have to say they did look quite good on their pale magnolia wall. Luckily they didn't ask me any further details of my time spent out in the bush, because at that time I knew very little about it. They moved away from me a few feet and then nodded in turn, whispering to each other until finally the lady of the house asked the price of the smaller one.

"It's only fifty bucks to you guys..." I said nervously in

my new fake Aussie drawl, while throwing them both a wide and probably quite gormless Bob Monkhouse smile. I must have sounded so incredibly dodgy that they probably hadn't a clue where I was from.

"Yeah, okay mate, fair dinkum, we'll take it..." the man said, in broad Australian as though actually competing with me for the best Aussie accent. When I realised that I'd made my first sale I thought I might explode in sheer relief and happiness, but I just managed to contain myself. The woman briefly disappeared and returned with a crisp new fifty dollar note. I hadn't seen one of these before, and it was the most beautiful thing I'd ever touched in my life. I stepped out of the house as though walking on air. I was ecstatic and felt hugely boosted by this sale, which sadly would only make me a measly $15 after the cost of the painting was deducted, but it was a sale nevertheless, and an example to myself of how it could be done.

Twilight fell quickly and preceded a calm, warm and very clear night. I frequently saw jet airliners directly above me flying quite low, crossing the wide, starry sky when landing and taking off from Sydney's Kingsford Smith airport, the navigation lights on their wingtips twinkling brightly as they passed; red port, green starboard, with white to the front and rear. Every few minutes plane loads of excited people were arriving in Australia, many of them no doubt with some real concrete plans, and others like me having none at all. More than once I thought that perhaps I should go home as planned in three weeks when my ticket dictated, and when my six week tourist visa expired.

In the open porch of one house I saw an enormous spider with a fat hairy body perched in the top left corner above the front door. It was as big as my hand and appeared to be a tarantula, or similar. When the door was opened by a rotund and much tanned middle-aged man, I pointed up at it and commented, and he just glanced around and said, casually:

"Oh yeah, that's a tarantula alright," as he then turned back to look at me and my folder. I expected him to reach for a broom and start whacking it but he did nothing. He wasn't interested in the paintings either, but before he shut the door he gave me some advice that for some reason stuck with me: "It's a long road, but you'll get there in the end with hard work…"

As I passed some of the houses I could see into the brightly lit front rooms at the apparently perfect domestic family life inside. Perhaps a father, a mother, a child or two, maybe also a family pet was running around. I saw real warmth inside some of these houses and I wondered just for an instant if I would ever have such a happy family of my own.

I knocked on the front doors of dozens of these large houses right up until the time came for me to find my rendezvous point again. I raved for more than half an hour in one house before the occupants finally declined to buy anything. Why didn't they tell me they were not interested in the first bloody place? This was clearly every salesperson's nightmare.

I failed to make another sale and was temporarily unsure of my location (never admit to being 'lost', it's an old aviator's motto) until I stumbled quite by chance on the same street corner I'd been dumped at two hours before. Ten minutes late, Dave couldn't hide an obvious look of disappointment when I told him I'd only made one sale. I am not a naturally talkative person, and trying to be so when selling the paintings was not easy for me. But I'd seen that night that it *was* possible. Not only that, but how good did it feel when I made a sale? It was a fantastic feeling.

One of the other two passengers in the car hadn't sold anything and I never saw him again, but the other one had made three sales, earning him $50, or so he said. As we weaved in and out of the night time traffic back to Bondi Junction I decided to give the paintings business another try, and maybe until the end of the week. Even if I only made $15 a night at least it was better than nothing. What else could I do?

The next night I was once again back in the wide, vacant suburban streets of Sydney knocking on doors with renewed determination. This time I sold three paintings, each with a broader Aussie accent and wider profit margin than the last, and made the glorious sum of $60. Not bad for two hours work. But I continued to find it very difficult. It was hard work talking with fake exuberance for two hours or more, in a happy and lively manner which was necessary to promote the paintings and make sales, and to do it repeatedly at every single doorstep. You had to be crisp and fresh each time a door was opened, dozens if not hundreds of times a night. In order to help generate the necessary ebullience I decided just before the third night's work to call in at the pub on the way. I threw back two double whiskies in quick succession before climbing the stairs to the office.

Less than an hour later I was standing in people's doorways being very loud and loquacious, widening the profit margins even further and making a modest number of sales but with $30 or $40 on each one. Listening to my accent you might think I'd lived in Australia all my life rather than just over three weeks. The best nightly total I managed in that first week was four paintings, pocketing $120 profit in one night. I now had over $300 in my wallet, which was a glorious sum of money. Things were looking up.

WARNERS AVENUE, NORTH BONDI

"We're Scientologists…"

I searched again in the paper, this time for my own place to live. I had finally taken the not-so-tactful hints that I couldn't live under a complete stranger's stairs forever. I had some money now too, so this brought with it some much needed freedom. I decided that I had to live close to the office, either within walking distance or on a reliable bus route, so I searched around the Bondi area. Eventually I found a room on the top floor of a large old tenement house at 54 Warners Avenue, North Bondi. It was quite near Bondi Junction and the office, but it was also ideal because it was close to the beach, some shops and a few fast-food restaurants.

I was shown around the house by a tall chap in his late twenties who had very greasy and straggly shoulder-length, dark hair which hung like rats' tails from beneath a wide-brimmed brown leather hat; a real life brown-hatter. He looked a bit like Mick Fleetwood from *Fleetwood Mac,* and I never saw him without his hat on. Maybe he showered with it on, if he even did shower, which I doubt, hence the lank greasiness. The rent was $45 a week, in advance, with a $90 bond to be paid when moving in. I took it without hesitation because of the location, and suddenly I found a large proportion of my money was gone again.

Within minutes of moving in, there was a loud and confident knock at the door of my top floor room. The man with the hat and a woman a few years younger than him stood in the doorway.

"We've made some tea, want some?" she said, with a pleasant smile and a slight feminine tilt of her head. The man then turned around, and in clear anticipation of me following them, they both walked in line down the stairs towards the kitchen, with me running to catch up. Green tea was made, with no milk, and the three of us sat down at the kitchen table. They introduced themselves as Mandy and Phil. I gave them my name and there were some happy handshakes all round. Mandy was wearing an ankle-length, flower-pattern, cotton dress and had long, thick, shoulder-length curly brown hair. She had pretty blue-green eyes and freckles and was a good-looking woman apart from the quite thick moustache on her top lip and pea-sized mole in the middle of her right cheek, which had a clump of black hair growing from the centre giving it the uncanny appearance of a tiny desert island with palm trees swaying in the breeze. She looked like she sweated a lot too. For some strange reason I immediately imagined that she would probably be very sweaty 'below stairs'.

"We're scientologists…" Phil suddenly blurted out between long gulps of tea. They both smiled at one another widely and very toothily like Donny and Marie Osmond, as though they'd just given me some really good news.

"Really?" I replied, utterly clueless as usual, trying my very best to fake some sincerity as much as I could. I remembered a piece of priceless advice someone once gave me: 'always be sincere, even if you have to fake it'.

"Yes, we were just discussing you, weren't we Mand?" Mandy just nodded slightly, almost imperceptibly, her mug of tea obscuring the bottom half of her face.

"Yes we think you should have an audit. I'd be happy to do it with you now, no pressure though eh?" Mandy put down her tea and looked across at me, clearly seeing a bewildered expression forming on my face.

"It's just a chat, to help resolve issues you might have, there's nothing to worry about…" Mandy said, smiling up at Phil. "Phil can do it here, now, can't you Phil?" as she stood up, pushing her chair back under the table.

Just then a small, thick-set, bearded man in his late twenties strode into the kitchen with quick determined steps and stopped at the sink. I hadn't been introduced and assumed he also lived somewhere in the house.

"Hi Angus!" Phil said to the man, smiling, "We're just setting Jonathan up for an audit; we still haven't done *you* yet have we?"

Angus was standing facing the sink running a tap but then turned around quickly: "I don't want anything to do with that load of shit!" just as he rolled his eyes and smiled across at me before turning back to the sink. He filled a tall glass with water and left the room briskly without saying another word. Phil laughed a kind of nervous, insincere laugh before commenting:

"Angus! Huh! He's a laugh isn't he? I'll get him one day!"

"I'll leave you both to it then," Mandy said as she picked up her mug and followed Angus out of the kitchen.

Phil stood up and shut the door. He sat down and looked intently into my eyes across the table.

"Try to relax. Empty your mind. I want you to think of something that really affected you in the past. A major event, something you have since regretted or wished had never happened. Something important that upset you, an incident, an encounter, maybe?"

There was a very uncomfortable silence. I was sitting at a filthy kitchen table in a dreary house with a complete stranger who was asking me some deeply personal questions. What on earth was he getting at? What should I say? I tried to think of answers. I thought about how much I regretted sitting down at the table with this idiot, but I realised this might not be quite what he was looking for. Then I thought about how much I'd hated getting acne on my face and shoulders when I was a teenager. Would that do? It was very important to me at the time. Then I thought about how I'd cocked up most of my school exams. Would that do? Then what about how I'd left a girlfriend behind in England?

"It could be a death in the family or something equally tragic…" Phil said, breaking my thoughts, clearly seeing me struggle. I didn't want to give this man anything remotely personal. Imagine if I had? I could be revealing secrets I never wanted to reveal, some of my innermost thoughts that should stay private forever. There were endless possibilities for ridicule, or even ultimately for blackmail. It was just too much! No, I had to give him *something*, but nothing *too* personal.

"My budgie died in my arms..." I finally announced, looking down, with a slightly quivering tone in my voice, followed by a very doleful frown with some worried and over-emphasised hand-wringing thrown in for good effect.

"Yes, yes, go on..." Phil replied, seeming very keen to extract more.

"Yes, his name was Skippy. He was my first pet. He died in my hands actually."

"Oh dear, what happened to him Jonathan?" Phil asked in a low voice, sounding quite sincere. There was a slight pause before I replied.

"He got a bad case of the shits. Really massive shits actually, big wide ones, and from such a tiny arse. I think he must have literally shat himself to death..."

I had to look down again, desperately trying to force back a smile. I coughed a little to cover up a tiny, accidental chuckle that escaped through my tightly clenched teeth. Phil must have mistaken this for an eruption of sadness because I then felt a reassuring hand on my left shoulder across the table.

"It's okay, it's good, it's good to let this out..."

"He was everything to me, he really was. I'd had him through all my teenage years. I'd even given him a second name."

"What was that, Jonathan?" Phil asked, with what sounded like some genuine sincerity and gentleness in his voice.

"I called him Skippy Keep..." The room fell quiet again. You could have heard a knitting needle drop onto the filthy and very sticky linoleum floor. I felt Phil's hand squeeze my shoulder again.

"What happened to Skippy Keep then, Jonathan?" Another lengthy and very awkward silence followed until I finally worked out very carefully in my head what to say in reply, as though I was being interviewed by the police.

"I buried him in a little cardboard box in the front garden. I put a cross over his grave and everything."

"This has clearly affected you. Have you discussed this event before, with anyone else?"

"No. No I haven't. This is the first time," which was true, as was the whole story, but who would really have been interested in the death of my budgerigar anyway?

"You need to use this event and move on from it, build on it, turn it into a positive. It's great you've told me about it though. This is really good for you, you do know that don't you?"

"Well, yes, thanks."

"Do you feel better?"

"Yes I do…" I replied, finding it very easy to lie, and still puzzled by the whole thing.

"I think we'll break here. We've had a great first audit, even though it was quite brief, and I hope now that you will pick up from here and move on from it. We'll have another one very soon, eh?" He continued giving me some wonderful platitudes the chair of any modern day business meeting would be proud of. I simply nodded repeatedly, glad to be getting away. It all seemed very creepy. One single thought filled my head: *What a load of bollocks.*

The next night was a Saturday, and after a long day lying around on the wonderful Bondi beach dipping in and out of the water body surfing, I called into the pub just before work as usual. A reasonable night followed and I sold three paintings for quite a decent profit, so at least I was flush again. Work finished at ten o'clock and as everyone in the office dispersed to go home Dave indicated very subtly for me to stay behind with a gentle wag of an index finger. He then shut the door and took out a large bag of green matter from a desk drawer and some cigarette papers. A couple of cigarettes were broken open onto his desk and mixed with the green matter, and then he joined several cigarette papers together. There were three other people present as well as Dave and me, and we all looked on as though we were watching a surgeon performing a complex operation.

A huge, thick joint about eight inches in length was then

passed around the office, the air of which began to fill quickly with very dense and quite distinctive, sweet-smelling cannabis smoke. Some music was put on and I recognised it as Jean-Michel Jarre, though I couldn't remember the title. The notes began to float around the office and bounce gently off the walls and into my head. After a few minutes I realised I was quite stoned. Dave commented loudly and with some very direct tactlessness that he could smell whiskey on my breath every night. I was alarmed and initially embarrassed by this but he seemed to think it was a curiosity, as though it had caused me to be more interesting to him, along with my stories about travelling and recent experiences of working in Israel and Germany.

After an hour we all left the office and went our separate ways. I decided to hang around Bondi Junction for a while to watch a pretty decent band I had discovered playing in one of the pubs. I was aware that I was probably walking around looking like an old *Thunderbirds* puppet, because my legs and arms felt very strange and seemed to be floating about all on their own. Not only that I think I was smiling constantly like a brainless idiot.

I spent some time in the pub watching the band and leaning on some soft furnishings near the bar until I realised what I was actually leaning on was a small oriental gentleman who never once complained. Perhaps the dear little chap was expecting something more?

I caught a late bus for the short journey down to Bondi and then stopped off at a pizza place I'd discovered overlooking the beach. I ordered a large chicken and mushroom pizza and carried it back to the house on Warners Avenue. It was a warm night and I had suddenly acquired a terrible and overpowering case of the munchies. It was by this time very late so I let myself in by the front door as quietly as I could and found the whole house was in total darkness. I walked into the kitchen and turned on the light.

I'd only previously seen cockroaches when on family holidays to the Spanish island of Majorca. They would be lying dead singly by the hotel pool or in the water, drowned. When I switched on the kitchen light that night I saw hundreds of the things, probably thousands, ranging in size from very small to a couple of inches long with some as big as mice, scurrying away into their dark hide holes on the kitchen work surface, across the floor and into all the cupboards. Large dark brown scaly cockroaches with long antennae and spiky legs seemed to completely occupy the kitchen, the same ones which had obviously been unseen during daylight hours. It was like the set of some jungle reality game show. I really hated the damned things too, cockroaches I mean, not jungle game shows.

COQUETTES AND COCKROACHES

"Pizza? I love pizza!"

I sat down at the round wooden kitchen table, and I noticed the blue square patterned Formica top was cracked and peeling around the edges revealing the plywood underneath. I placed the pizza box on the table, in the centre, deliberately away from the edges, and began eating. I looked around nervously, constantly on guard against cockroaches. I felt as though I was surrounded by a living kitchen, where the walls and cupboards were alive and breathing, always moving around and watching me. I didn't mind mice, or spiders, but I just felt terribly uneasy about cockroaches. They seemed to move so quickly and could wriggle in and out of the tiniest places, and of course not forgetting the most surprising fact of all, that they could fly. An occasional one scurried past my feet on the floor, and I could see clusters of small brown ones in the corners of the room, writhing and crawling about all over one another. The place was infested with them. In the UK even a few sightings could warrant a visit from the pest controllers.

I finished my lovely pizza and left the kitchen for my bedroom upstairs, treading carefully on each creaking step in the poor light in case I stood on anything wriggling and crunchy. My bedroom was dark and I shuddered to think what I might find when I turned on the light. It was quite a large room with a high ceiling and an old, sunken, single bed against one wall. A bare light bulb dangled forlornly from the centre of the ceiling, and a pair of once bright but now tatty and faded flower patterned curtains hung very sullenly at each side of the window. When I switched on the light thankfully it didn't seem to have the same effect as in the kitchen, at least not at first. There were no signs of any scurrying insects and it seemed that I was safe. I assumed in my naivety that because I was on the top floor the creatures might not be able to reach my room. It was still quite a warm night so I undressed and sat up in bed, leaning against the cool bare wall.

I took out a book and began to read. The room seemed strangely and suspiciously cockroach free. I grew tired very quickly and couldn't concentrate on my book so I turned off the ceiling light in favour of the less bright lamp on the tiny table by my bed and readied myself for sleep. I could feel myself drifting away so I turned this light off after a few minutes. I lay on my back in the dark and there was some soft, white light from the window casting a pale, ethereal glow right across the room. The days' events passed through my mind. I'd wandered down to the beach after breakfast as usual at about noon in a new and wonderful daily ritual and spent long periods of time in the sea. I'd caught some fantastic waves, and one or two were timed just perfectly so they dragged me all the way up the beach, a hundred yards or more. I was learning to recognise a good wave, and you could tell immediately when you'd caught a great one, because it felt just like it had physically grabbed you very tightly around the waist and wouldn't let go. It was exhilarating and utterly addictive.

The effects of the joint and the slow digestion of the heavy, doughy pizza were sending me into a deep, drifting sleep. I felt very alone, but at that moment it didn't seem to matter, I was quite content with my world. Warners Avenue was silent apart from the occasional vehicle passing by in the street below, so I closed my eyes and slowly I was gone.

I must have been asleep when it started. I sensed something light, touching me over the thin bed sheet, tapping me over and over, up and down the full length of my body quite at random and then finally on my face. It sounded like the beginning of rain falling on a tent, a gentle pitter-patter that was growing in intensity. Was I dreaming about being in a tent, perhaps pitched somewhere on the beautiful Derbyshire hills, with a shower just starting? I didn't panic at first, but I was awake enough to reach for the lamp by the bed.

As the switch clicked loudly and the light filled the room, in an instant I could see exactly what was responsible for the tapping sensations on the bed. Lines of cockroaches were climbing the wall next to me and were trying to cross the ceiling. They were falling from directly above my bed, dropping onto me like paratroopers or cliff divers, one after the other, until the last one had landed on my face near my mouth.

I immediately sprang out of bed, frantically brushing the filthy insects from me. One had become caught up in my hair and I could feel it wriggling away trying to free itself as I dared to brush it with my fingers. I reached for my copy of the *Sydney Morning Herald* and rolled it up into the shape of a long paper club. I leapt around the room taking swipes at the insects, and I believe I did hit one or two, but most simply disappeared into the ubiquitous cracks in the floor and walls. I was astonished at just how fast they could run in order to avoid being squished. They have an almost supernatural ability to evade being clubbed to death, and it turns out there is a good reason for this. Their back legs can apparently move quite independently of their tiny brain, and when threatened they can sense the smallest change in air pressure such as when a rolled up newspaper is wielded clumsily towards them. Their back legs automatically kick the insect to safety completely bypassing the brain and the need to make a decision about it. The whole manoeuvre is therefore conducted in a split second, so we lumbering humans, therefore, have little chance against them.

Cockroaches were scurrying across the floor in every direction, running over my naked feet apparently not frightened of physical contact, and I saw others crawling around on and *inside* my bed. This was just a nightmare come true for me, and I spent the next desperate hour hunting cockroaches all around the room, frantically trying to block their many entry routes with bits of crunched up newspaper. Eventually with the insect numbers virtually reduced to nil I returned to bed when sheer exhaustion forced me to do so. I lay like a plank on the very edge of the bed, as though I'd just had an argument with an imaginary partner, with the light staying on. I kept an eye open for insects as best I could for as long as I could, but finally I very slowly drifted off to sleep.

I spent all the next day on the beach as usual. The sun was hot and unrelenting, the skin on my face felt tight and stretched like the surface of a drum, and my hair was very dry and straw-like from the ocean salt and sand from the beach. Parts of my body were beginning to deepen in colour and in some places actually appeared to look and feel like very dark brown shoe leather. I wasn't using any sun-tan lotion, I never did.

I continued to spend hours in the water chasing the elusive 'dream wave', catching the occasional one before returning to the warm sand. I drifted in and out of sleep lying on the beach, listening to my Walkman. Between songs from my headphones the sound of children laughing and playing on the beach in the near distance was very soothing and reminded me of many carefree childhood family holidays spent on English beaches in Dorset or Norfolk.

I knew that if I wanted to I could work that night, even though it was a Sunday, and I had originally decided that I wouldn't, but as the afternoon passed I realised I would have little else to do. I arrived in the office at the usual time of seven o'clock. There was only one other person apart from myself who turned up that night. Rich was a New Zealander, from Auckland, and I'd noticed he was always at work, as I was. Dave took both of us in his car to an outer suburb of Sydney, where I did quite well, but nowhere near as well as Rich.

It was a good job I had decided to go to work that night. At the end of the evening Dave announced that he was looking for two reliable people who were good sellers to take a car and some paintings later that week on a country trip away from the city for a few days, to see how much could be sold. There were other rival teams across Sydney selling paintings in direct competition and the market was rapidly becoming saturated. It was time to find some new and fertile ground in which to sell. Rich and I could both drive, so in the absence of anyone

34

else Dave offered us the job. To celebrate, Dave then took out his usual bag of cannabis and rolled a joint, passing it between the three of us. He also took out a large bottle of Jack Daniels from his drawer and poured three glasses with a generous amount in each, handing them around.

"You'll probably go on Tuesday, or Wednesday, okay?" Dave raised his glass and the three of us chinked them together before we took a sip of the sweet, deep-red bourbon. Dave knocked his back in two or three quick gulps and then rose to his feet and began tidying up the office. It was clearly time for us to leave.

I collected my chicken and mushroom pizza and arrived back at Warners Avenue quite early, at least well before midnight. I was surprised to find there was quite a lot of activity in the house. I saw Phil crossing the street and in through the front door just before me, his wide-brimmed hat covering his greasy rats' tails hair which flopped about on his shoulders. I passed Angus on the stairs, and he glanced at me quickly, shaking his head, without saying a word. I went straight upstairs to my room to eat my pizza, bypassing the cockroach kitchen. Turning on the ceiling light I chased away a few cockroaches from my bed, clearing a space to sit down. I was getting used to sharing my room with a menagerie of local wildlife. After a few moments and several heavenly mouthfuls of pizza there was a knock on the door to my room.

I opened it and standing in the doorway in front of me was a gorgeous young woman in her late teens with a brown bottle of Tia Maria in one hand. I vaguely remembered seeing her on a couple of occasions in the house a few days before but I'd not really spoken to her. She was so young and pretty I'd assumed she was with someone.

"Hi," she said, smiling and as soon as she spoke I could tell she'd been drinking heavily, most probably from the bottle she had in her hand. Her speech was very slurred, her eyes were rolling around in her head like a doll's and she was swaying slightly at the door, as though she was standing on the deck of a rolling ship.

"Hi, how are you?" I said in reply. "Are you okay?" I asked, smiling at her, bending over slightly to get a better look at her face. She stepped inside the room and immediately confirmed my initial suspicions because she clearly found it very difficult to walk in a straight line or even remain vertical.

"I wondered," she said, moving over towards my bed, "I wondered if I could sleep with you tonight?" she said, as she sat down on the bed, or more accurately fell onto it, narrowly missing my pizza which I was still trying to eat. I was taken completely by surprise at this marvellous proposition from someone so lovely, and was pleasantly shocked and flattered. I'd never been quite lucky enough to be in this situation before, so I didn't really know what to do. I looked around and for a moment I couldn't believe it was happening. She was certainly slim and gorgeous with thick blonde hair and beautiful brown eyes, and very pretty. I didn't even know her name or anything about her. Why was she wanting to do this, and with a complete stranger?

In a fit of ridiculously chivalrous behaviour, and no doubt some men would probably say stupidity, I took hold of her arms and hauled her up off the bed. I could smell the Tia Maria on her breath and noticed more than half the bottle had already been drunk. I sealed my pizza back in its box as best I could and tried to get her attention before carrying her towards the door.

"Where's your room, which one?" I asked her, to which she replied

"Downstairs, second floor...why?" as I put an arm around her slim waist and half dragged her along the hallway. She was indeed lovely and I could smell some gorgeous flower-scented perfume on her soft skin she was so close to me. I virtually carried her down the stairs and all the way to her door. I opened it and left her inside on her bed before shutting the door quickly and retreating back towards the stairs. It did occur to me to take advantage of her, of course it did, as it would any heterosexual male, and at least several times too. But this would have clearly been a very one-sided union, if indeed she would have managed to stay awake throughout, which I doubted.

On my way back to the stairs I saw Mandy on the second floor landing wandering unsteadily towards me. She looked like she'd been drinking too, or something, as she had a wide gormless smile which stretched right across her face like the Joker in *Batman*. She stopped at the foot of the stairs as I passed her, and just for a moment I felt as though she wanted to speak to me, but I didn't give her the opportunity. My pizza was still waiting for me, I had a serious case of the munchies, and if I didn't get back to my food quickly the native wildlife would almost certainly eat it for me.

I sat back on my bed and happily resumed placating my munchies with the pizza. After a few bites back into it there was another knock at the door. I assumed it was the girl again, and so I decided I couldn't be bothered to get up. Perhaps I'd let her stay after all?

"Come in!" I shouted across the room through my pizza, thoroughly enjoying my food. When the door opened I saw not the young girl but Mandy standing in the doorway, leaning on the door frame with one arm stretched above her head like Marlene Dietrich leaning on a lamp post. She was wearing a bright flowery dress, the hem of which was well above her knees, and it was one that I hadn't noticed before. It didn't look quite right though somehow, whether it was the dope I'd smoked earlier I wasn't sure, but I couldn't help thinking she looked like she'd wrapped herself in a pair of curtains, like Scarlet O'Hara in *Gone with the Wind,* the fabric was so bright and garish. But it was touching her figure in all the right places, and from a safe distance across the room she did look rather nice, if a little bit scruffy and unkempt.

She then walked straight into the room, shutting the door loudly behind her. I didn't say anything; I hadn't a clue what she wanted. In a few moments it all became quite clear, and it wasn't food she was looking for.

"Pizza? I *love* pizza," she said, and sat down on the bed next to me, very close, staring. She helped herself to a thin slice from the box open on my lap with her right hand, and then shoved her left hand firmly between my legs underneath the pizza box. She took one bite from the end of her floppy piece of pizza and then without warning thrust the rest of her pizza into my face, forcing me to take a bite from it. She giggled loudly and then picked up the pizza box and threw it onto the bedside table out the way.

"You're very brown aren't you?" she said as she suddenly lunged forward without another word, forcing me backwards with both hands, pressing me firmly up against the wall. She then started slobbering all over me like an over anxious Labrador reunited with its owner, her long thin tongue making deep, searching sweeps inside my mouth as though she was counting my teeth with it. I still had quite a lot of pizza squelching around in there so I tried to swallow it down while also trying not to suffocate; her mouth was clamped hard onto my face like a clam. Her hands were around the back of my head and she began pulling it towards her, gripping it so tightly her fingers were beginning to rip at my hair and hurt my scalp.

Suddenly, and to my great surprise she started gyrating about on top of me, up and down and side to side, faster and faster. Then she released her grip for a moment, raised both her arms and pulled the dress off over her head from the bottom in one quick movement. I am always impressed when I see women do this; it seems to me to be quite a distinct skill to disrobe in one single manoeuvre like that. I tried to remove a t-shirt in that manner once and almost dislocated a shoulder.

She resumed her stance, French kissing and dribbling spit all over me while I lay there in shock. Her long greasy hair was flailing around all over my face but I caught fleeting glimpses of her body and it did look very nice; an off-white frilly bra, with some nice sized boobs bobbing around inside, and pale blue panties.

"I hear you had a good audit..." she said in between licks and catching her breath.

"Er... yes..." I replied, still unable to move. I decided I

might start taking part and so I clasped my hands onto her waist and gripped it tightly. Suddenly as I did so she let out some deep and very strange groaning sounds as though she was trying to cough, and at first I thought she might be choking or suffering an asthma attack before she then started screaming and shuddering, shaking all over like she'd just stepped into a cold shower.

In a few brief moments she stopped moving completely and sat up. She was sweating and was extremely breathless. Just as I was getting interested she climbed off me and looked around for her dress, which was hanging half off the bed beside her. She stood up and slipped it back over her head.

"Yes Phil said you made some good progress in your audit, which is great." She resumed a conversation in her broad Aussie accent as though nothing had happened. "You shouldn't think that it's all nonsense, like Angus does, it isn't eh, it really works…"

I sat up, a little confused and still fully clothed in jeans and my white *Doncaster Aero Club* t-shirt. She tidied her hair with both hands and looked at me very seriously with a quizzical expression forming on her face. In her usual Aussie drawl she then said:

"Got any fags?"

THE COUNTRY TRIP

"Good heads, eh?"

I barely knew Rich before we were thrown together on the trip, and we'd only briefly communicated with each other on a handful of occasions before then. He was softly spoken and patrician in his manner, almost effeminate with some delicate and considered mannerisms. He was slim but not athletic, and spoke with a very broad New Zealand accent, which is similar to the Australian accent but the vowel sounds are even more clipped and pronounced. 'I don't really have an icksent do I?' he said to me when I remarked on it, not long after we first met. Even among Australians it was quite noticeable.

Rich was given the car keys first so he drove us both in the lumbering white Ford Fairmont carefully and smoothly out of Sydney, north on the Pacific Highway. We drove across the Harbour Bridge and then past the wonderful Ku-Ring Gai Chase National Park winding ever higher up through some densely-forested hills and beautiful red-brown rock formations. Further to the west I could see the Blue Mountains in the distance. I was hugely impressed by what I was seeing. I'd been in Australia almost a month and this was the first genuine countryside I'd seen. This was the real Australia, not the Harbour Bridge or the Opera House, but this, the open country, and I felt a tremendous surge of interest in it.

West of Newcastle we turned inland on Highway 15 and passed through Maitland and then onto Singleton. We'd been driving for almost three hours when we decided to change drivers. It was the first time I'd driven in Australia. Highway 15 from Singleton to Muswellbrook was a good place to start; a long wide straight road with very few driving challenges or problems. The weather was superb with some fluffy, fair-weather cumulus clouds floating slowly overhead like generous portions of pure white candyfloss. I enjoyed the driving; it was easy and it was fun, and at least the Aussies drive on the correct side of the road!

It was now April and almost the end of summer. Everywhere looked very dry and appeared more so the further we drove inland. Occasionally I saw wild kangaroos, some noticeably quite large, hopping around in the fields and close to the road. It was the first time I'd fully realised kangaroos really do populate the Australian countryside in that way and they weren't merely symbolic, mythical creatures used to attract tourists. Some lay in the road itself and by the sides of the road with various degrees of physical trauma from being struck by vehicles and in differing stages of decomposition. Occasionally high up in the branches of gum trees there would be a ball of fur visible about the size of a football clinging onto the trunk of the tree, or perhaps sitting on a branch, not doing a great deal. A second look would confirm these immobile blobs to be koala bears, looking incredibly cute and somehow unreal just plonked in the trees as they were.

When we reached Muswellbrook we stopped for a while. I parked the car nose-in at a sixty degree angle in-line with others in the wide main street. Parking at such an angle saved so much space and ensured many more cars could stop compared to the European method of parallel parking. But these streets seemed almost as broad as they were long, designed with forethought, perhaps anticipating traffic use that would become more than just the occasional horse and cart. The streets in the town were like those in North America, wide open and clear. We were heading for Tamworth that day, and it was already mid-afternoon. We stopped long enough for a toilet break and a drink before setting out again.

Rich and I exchanged life histories to date. Rich seemed impressed by my travelling experiences so far. He had only made it there from Auckland, a mere four hour plane ride away, and not that much of a cultural change to Australia. I also found out how Rich made such spectacular sales, rarely selling less than half a dozen paintings each night. He used a pencil and a notepad and pretended he was deaf and dumb. My first thoughts were how immoral this seemed, relying to such a huge extent on sympathy for sales. It was all so very fraudulent too, in my humble opinion.

But Rich told me of the funnier side to his selling exploits and the many unguarded conversations he'd heard amongst his victims when deciding whether or not to buy a painting. 'Look at 'im, he looks so thin…' and 'The poor bastard', and 'At least he's trying', and so on, unaware that he could hear every touching word. On rare occasions his apparent condition was really put to the test; repeated personal insults were thrown directly at him behind his back in order to provoke a response, but Rich said he always held it together. He was a psychology graduate, or so he said, and he claimed he knew something of how the human mind worked. I thought it was quite outrageous and at no time was I even tempted to give it a try, despite Rich insisting it would work well, as it did for him. I feared there was a real danger that I would weaken, in seriousness, or even if I heard such comments I might simply crack by being unable to control a smile or a giggle, or worse. When you absolutely cannot laugh, as in lecture times at school, sometimes the most elementary joke or simple one-liner can cause side-splitting hysterics. No, I thought, I just couldn't trust myself, in addition to the fact that I really did think it was quite immoral.

As we drove through the neat little towns of Aberdeen and Scone, north of Muswellbrook, the railway line followed the road closely and we stayed on Highway 15 until we arrived in Tamworth in the early evening. We found a campsite and booked into a small caravan. I didn't have a lot of money left so when Rich suggested we try some selling that night, I agreed immediately, so just as darkness fell we trudged off into the clean wide streets of Tamworth, half a dozen paintings under our arms.

Doorstep receptions were quite positive, more so than in the Sydney suburbs. People were generally very friendly, and many seemed more than a little curious to find an artist at their door. Clearly they had not been customers of such sales tactics before. We both agreed to return to the caravan at nine o'clock, and when we did so we had sold four paintings each. Rich made huge profits on his sales of around fifty dollars each, but I was a little more conservative and made a hundred bucks that night. Not bad for two hours work though.

The next day we set out much later than planned. We didn't reach Armidale until after lunch. The town was small but looked a good place to stop with neat suburban streets and prosperous looking houses, so we found another campsite and booked in. After a sandwich and coffee we each wandered into the streets with a folder of priceless Australian art under our arms. It was a warm afternoon and I didn't really feel much like working. Despite a positive reception at most houses that I knocked at I didn't have much success. I imagined Rich with his pad and pencil: '*Hello. My name is Richard. I am a mute. I can neither hear you nor speak to you. I have painted these pictures and I wondered if you could help me out by buying one or two of them...*'

After making three unremarkable sales with a moderate profit on each one I began to relax and knocked on the front door of a smart wooden house in Skinner Street. An attractive blonde in some skin-tight blue jeans answered the door and without really listening to me she quickly ushered me inside. I gave her my name and some of the sales patter but she just sat cross-legged on the polished-wood living room floor and indicated for me to do the same. I sensed a warm atmosphere along with quite a prominent aroma of recent cannabis smoke. After explaining how the bright Australian light was ideal for painting pictures, the young woman, probably in her mid-twenties, suddenly said:

"Do you like to smoke?" just as she leaned across the floor, reaching for an object from behind a chair. As she stretched out on all fours I couldn't help but notice that she had the nicest backside I'd seen in a long time.

"Yeah, sure..." I replied, just beginning to understand what she meant, and being slightly distracted by the view. The woman pulled out a bamboo tube about eight inches long with a round base and a steel pipe sticking out at an angle on one side. It was the first time I'd ever seen a 'bong', and it wouldn't be the last. She then placed a small wooden bowl on the floor between us into which she crushed several green lumps the size of thumb nails from a plastic bag and then ripped open a Marlboro cigarette. She mixed it all together with the fingers of both hands very carefully as though making pastry, and then took a generous pinch in the index finger and thumb of her left hand. Holding the bong with her right hand she stuffed the mixture into the cone shape at the end of the pipe sticking out from the bamboo. She lit it and puffed on it thoughtfully for a few moments like Sherlock Holmes pondering a difficult problem, and there was a hissing and a strange bubbling noise before she passed it across the floor. I realised then that there was water inside the tube when I lifted it up and almost spilt the contents all over myself. The woman then exhaled in a long controlled blow of smoke which reached the ceiling like the tall billowing cloud from a nuclear bomb. She smiled at me just as I fixed the top of the bong over my mouth to form a tight seal. I inhaled deeply and could see the mixture glow red in the small brass cone as I did so.

This process was repeated several times and I slowly became detached from reality and increasingly relaxed. My host began to look lovelier than ever and her warm convivial manner made me think I'd known her all my life. I told her about Rich and our joint expedition selling paintings. She didn't seem concerned, and wasn't the least interested in the pictures. Waves of tetrahydrocannabinol, or THC, the active ingredient of the cannabis, began to fill my blood through the lining of my lungs. It surged quickly up into my head with every heartbeat, settling gently in every cell of my brain.

It's probably appropriate at this point to explain in a little more detail some of the effects of THC, because I understand that not everyone will have tried cannabis. Imagine drinking a couple of large glasses of good quality single malt Scotch whisky quite quickly on an empty stomach when you've not had a drink for some time. You might find the room starts to spin and you become light headed and euphoric. It's likely that you may start talking nonsensical rubbish for a while, become a little giggly and develop a surge of interest in music followed by the desire to eat stodgy food like chips and pizza. You may also feel quite emotional and frisky too. After a few hours if you don't keep it up you will inevitably feel very tired and fall asleep, probably listening to your favourite music. That's what happens to me when I drink a good Scotch, and the parallels with cannabis are pretty close. Of course there are many varieties of cannabis as there is Scotch, but in my humble opinion that just about sums it up. I'm not advocating that you immediately go out to look for some cannabis and then throw away all your Scotch, far from it, but there really is nothing else to it, and no great mystery. But if you drink a bottle of Scotch every day there may be some adverse consequences to follow, similarly with regular and chronic use of cannabis. Moderation is the key, and as with most such things moderate use is something that has to be learnt. Sadly, some people find this difficult if not impossible at first, and I include myself in this. If you don't smoke you could always eat the stuff, either raw or in the form of cakes or biscuits, and this has a similar if slightly delayed effect. I remember once coming out of Gaza with a small slice of hash in my pocket that had just been given to me by some Palestinian guys at the beach. I was with a Dutch girl, Angelique, and we were so terrified of the soldiers at the Israeli checkpoint finding it that we broke it in half and swallowed it down all at once. We were completely out of it for days.

I looked around the room and the absurdities of my situation struck me quite suddenly and I began to smile to myself. Unable to resist it any longer I started to laugh out loud, while staring at the paintings on the floor.

"Good heads eh?" the woman said, smiling back at me, as she prepared to load another cone.

"Yes, yes it is good stuff isn't it?" I replied, sounding very

English and momentarily forgetting my Aussie accent. I looked around the room. Was I back in Israel? No, I wasn't, I was in Germany... no, no... I wasn't, I was in England. No, I was in Australia. *Australia?* What the hell was I doing in Australia? I looked around again. The bright afternoon sun filled the lovely room through a massive picture window and the broad shafts of light grew ever more distinct from the smoke we were exhaling, which climbed upwards in a continually rolling fog reminiscent of cigarette smoke through cinema projections. I suddenly felt quite wonderful and wanted to stay there forever. It seemed I'd found my Shangri-La in the warm sunshine and so I decided at that moment I would live there permanently with her in that lovely house.

The woman suddenly stood up and put the bong on a side table, shattering my daydream in an instant.

"I gotta go out for a few hours. Why don't you come back later and we'll have another smoke if you like?"

"Yeah, sure..." I replied, amazed at how composed the woman seemed to be after smoking so much. I felt as though I could hardly move, let alone stand up without falling over, and holding a reasonable conversation just seemed impossible. She, however, seemed entirely normal as she wandered about the house, picking up her keys and putting on her shoes. She looked incredibly sexy too, as her small but wonderfully unrestrained bosoms bounced around inside her t-shirt. With what seemed like a huge amount of self-control and a monumental effort I managed to put all the paintings back into my folder and shuffle towards the front door.

"See you later then eh? Bring Rich with you too. You can't miss this house eh; it's on Skinner Street, number four! Do you get it? Four Skinner Street? Foreskin-er Street!" and she laughed, probably more to herself than for my benefit. "I'm Barbara by the way... see you later then?"

I stepped out into the street and began walking in the general direction of the caravan park. By now I'd become quite good at navigating the anonymous Australian streets, despite the fact that I sincerely believed my natural sense of direction had dwindled to nothing since leaving the northern hemisphere. I found that my innate sense of where north was seemed to elude me repeatedly, or was it the fact that I was destroying it by addling my brain so much? But I'm not a homing pigeon, so surely the rapid transition from north to south wouldn't have any noticeable effect on me? It was probably nonsense, like the time when I was brushing my teeth in the bathroom at Warners Avenue the first night I was there, observing the water drain away down the plughole in an anti-clockwise direction. Great experiment, but I couldn't remember which way it went in the northern hemisphere, so it was pretty inconclusive. I could have sworn it went down clockwise the next time anyway.

The late afternoon sun was very pleasant on my face and I was filled with a marvellous sense of well-being. All was very well with the world. I unlocked the caravan and sat down inside. I turned on the small television and found it utterly compelling, even the adverts. Rich arrived back stating he was hungry and very quickly suggested we drive into the town for some food, which to me at that moment seemed like a brilliant idea.

Over a particularly wonderful omelette and chips from a chip shop I told Rich about Barbara and the invite back to her house later.

"I thought you were acting a bit weird," he said, smiling, sipping delicately and effeminately from a can of Coke, while chewing like a rabbit on a huge bowl of chips and mixed salad leaves. He told me he was a vegetarian and he said: 'Just look at a person eating a chicken leg with their bare hands and it's enough to put you off meat forever...'

After the meal we decided to work for just an hour before meeting back at the caravan in the hope of then finding Skinner Street. I was by this time sobering up a little and was looking forward to returning, but I still managed two quite decent sales. Rich sold four paintings in the space of an hour. I was back at the caravan first and when we set out on foot we found Skinner Street quite quickly, despite the fact it was almost dark.

Barbara answered the door and I immediately noticed she was not quite as light-hearted as she had been earlier in the afternoon. I then saw a man in the background, in the kitchen, and he looked as though he was cooking. Barbara made no reference to him. The three of us then sat at a dining table facing each other and the smoking ritual began again. The bong was placed on the table and then the small wooden bowl. Half a dozen lumps of cannabis plant heads were broken up into the bowl and then a Marlboro cigarette was dismantled with great care and reverence, and sprinkled into the bowl and mixed together. The first cone was packed and Barbara lit it and took a few puffs. There was little conversation, and the atmosphere in the house was somehow different, tense almost, and Barbara seemed edgy, frequently glancing towards the kitchen.

She and I smoked with great enthusiasm and the atmosphere began to lighten. We encouraged Rich to smoke quickly so he would catch us up, which he did. I thought again how pretty Barbara was. She was small and delicate with soft freckles across her nose and cheeks, wide eyes like deep pools of blue sky, and red-blonde hair in ringlets which balanced delicately on her shoulders. She occasionally scooped her hair back behind both ears alternately with one finger in an effortlessly sexy manner, the way only naturally sexy women can.

The room was dimly lit, but despite this after an hour of talking and smoking Barbara and I could clearly see that Rich was becoming unwell. He went very pale and quiet, his head occasionally dropped forwards and then finally he fell from his chair very heavily and landed on the floor in a crumpled heap. He lay on his side drawing his legs up to his chest like a baby with wind pains, mumbling something about the tobacco. His face actually looked quite weird and was an odd shade of pale green.

Barbara and I found this hilarious at first and with Rich's wide, tight, curly hair close around his head and face we joked that he looked like a little green spaceman or Leo Sayer having a very bad hair day. We both started making strange alien bleeping noises and I was almost literally pissing myself it was so funny. Rich then crawled past the table on all fours moaning and growling, demanding to know where the toilet was. To us he then became a little green space dog, and was the funniest thing I'd seen in years. Every time Rich spoke it sounded like he was barking at us, just like a dog, and it all seemed incredibly amusing. Poor Rich just looked as though he would die at any moment.

Suddenly a look of great seriousness swept over Barbara's face.

"We can't make too much noise, eh?" she said, anxiously looking towards the kitchen. The man had moved from there and along the hallway into a bedroom. He still hadn't been through to join us, or even to say hello. I didn't understand this. Who was he, and who did he think *we* were? Rich disappeared into the bathroom, still crawling, and was in there for quite some time. He missed two more cones actually, before I heard the toilet flush and he reappeared, looking ashen and drained.

"I gotta go..." he said, still crawling around on the floor, "I need to crash out...I think it was the tobacco..." he said in his Kiwi accent. "Are you staying or coming with me or what?" as he looked up at me, squinting as though staring at the midday sun. I wanted to stay, I never wanted to leave, but then Barbara spoke for me in a sudden and surprisingly serious tone:

"Yeah, it's late, eh..."

I felt a connection with Barbara that day. There was definitely something there. It had started the first time we'd met on that warm sunny afternoon, but just then in an instant it was broken. As Barbara held the front door open and said goodbye I noticed some bruises on the underside of both her arms for the first time. They looked like grip or grab marks.

"Thanks for a brilliant afternoon, and evening, Barbara..." I said. She smiled and looked directly at me with her big blue eyes:

"Look after yourself; I hope you find what you're looking

49

for." She kissed me lovingly on the lips, holding the kiss firmly and warmly for a few moments longer than necessary, and then looked down at her feet as she closed the door. It all seemed rather sad and final.

I virtually carried Rich a difficult half mile back to the caravan. It was a huge effort. I laid him down on his bed and sat watching television for a while. I couldn't get Barbara out of my mind. I wanted to go back, to see her, to make sure she was alright. It was as though she needed to be rescued from something, or someone. Then I fell asleep with the television blaring away in the corner.

QUEENSLAND

"Here's the mull bowl, give it a try..."

The next morning we sped through Glen Innes and didn't stop, as though we were in a pursuit, or being pursued. In fact it was around there that we gave a young hitchhiker a lift and deliberately played a trick on him. We held a conversation between the two of us which on reflection was rather stupid:

"Do you think the cops will catch us?"

"No, but you shouldn't have shot that second one that was just stupid..."

"I know but he was going for his gun, I had no choice."

"I guess so, but we need to get moving."

"There might be roadblocks too..." and so on, for quite some time. Luckily when the lad got out of the car quite hastily after an hour there were no phone boxes around, or else we could have been in serious trouble. He didn't say a single word to us though, the whole time he was in the car.

I wondered why the name Glen Innes seemed familiar. Then I remembered John Innes was written all over some large bags of garden compost I'd seen years before in my dad's greenhouse. I wondered if there was a possible family connection between the two names. Brothers John and Glen went their separate ways and one built a town in New South Wales and the other built a factory making compost. Unlikely. We turned right and headed for the coast.

The Gwydir Highway between Glen Innes and Grafton was a brilliant drive, a wide open road snaking through the Gibraltar Range National Park. Luckily it was largely traffic free, which made the journey so much quicker and more pleasurable. I was surprised at how few multi-lane motorways there were in Australia. Instead there were mainly single track roads with occasional overtaking lanes grafted onto them, where everyone suddenly went quite mad, hitting the gas hard as though for a few minutes they'd been dropped into an episode of *The Whacky Races*, desperately trying to get past slower vehicles in front.

At Grafton we made a quick stock-take before we had to make a decision. We were now quite close to Queensland and if we had more paintings with us we could have crossed over the border and tried our luck over there, but we just didn't have enough to make it worthwhile. After much discussion we decided to stay the night in Grafton and try to sell the remainder of the paintings while we were there. We found a campsite and a decent caravan before we ate in a nearby café. That night I marched off into the night with four paintings and Rich had five. These were all we had left, and we sold them in less than two hours.

The distances in Australia took some getting used to. We were still almost 400 miles or at least 650 kilometres away from Sydney and our selling was over. We had effectively finished work so I persuaded Rich that we should stay a final night in Port Macquarie, mainly to break up the journey, but also for me to see what the waves and the surfing was like there. We stopped briefly for a beer and a break in Coffs Harbour before resuming. We passed through the banana growing areas of New South Wales, and a place near Coffs called *The Big Banana*, which looked like some sort of banana-based theme park, though sadly we didn't pull over to take a closer look.

We stayed in a motel close to the estuary of the Hastings River and overlooking the sea in Port Macquarie where the ocean looked absolutely wonderful. I vowed to myself that one day I would return with my body board and try out the waves. We walked into the town that night and had quite a few beers, staying up much later than usual. It had been a good trip and I had thoroughly enjoyed seeing more of Australia.

In the morning once we had finally set off we only stopped very occasionally for fuel and toilet breaks, changing drivers each time. At six o'clock that night we finally reached the seemingly endless northern suburbs of Sydney and eventually crossed the Harbour Bridge. It was Sunday and we'd been away for four nights and five days. I felt strangely different as I drove the car up towards Bondi Junction. It suddenly dawned on me without really thinking about it that I was at last beginning to know my way around Sydney, as I drove the car from the bridge through the busy nightlife at King's Cross, past Rushcutter's Bay, Edgecliff, and finally to Bondi Junction. I didn't know many of the street names, but I could navigate across the city quite well. We left the car in the rear car park of the office as instructed and went our separate ways again.

I collected my usual pizza and when I entered my room at Warners Avenue I felt like Charlton Heston returning home from Rome in the movie *Ben Hur*. The window had been left partially open and leaves and other detritus had blown in across the floor and onto my bed giving it a long abandoned look, as though it had been unoccupied for years and not just a few days. I finished eating before I quickly gathered up the leaves and threw them back out the window. Then after forcing some cockroaches to flee I lay down on my bed feeling very tired. I wrote in my diary and read for a while. I thought of the last few days, the trip, Rich, the beautiful countryside I'd seen and the fact that I still wanted to see more. I also thought of Barbara in Armidale.

Very early the next morning I was surprised to be told there was a visitor at the front door asking for me. It was Dave. I couldn't even recall giving him my address.

"I'm relocating the business up north, to Brisbane. I'll have an office, cars, paintings, everything. You can come along too. Are you interested? Rich is coming with me." Dave smiled at me and started nodding slightly as he did so, emphasising the positive like a true salesman. I thought for a moment and then glanced around briefly at the cockroach infested tenement that was 54 Warners Avenue. What had I got to lose?

"Yeah, great. When do we go?" I said, expecting Dave to tell me maybe in a week's time or even two weeks.

"Well, how about now?" Dave replied, probably in full

knowledge that this would be a complete surprise. "I've spoken to Rich, and he's ready. There's no time like right now eh?"

I suspected Dave knew that I had no ties to Sydney, and if he'd spoken to Rich he must have known how much I'd enjoyed the country trip. It had been a great success financially for all concerned and we'd certainly proved we were good workers. But it meant a quick turn around and back on the road that day.

I terminated my lease with the house and because no damage was found in my room I collected my $90 bond from Phil. It was the last time I saw the house and the people in it. On a recent return trip to Australia I noticed the building had been completely demolished. The young girl at my door with the Tia Maria had apparently left very early the day after her encounter with me. I'd obviously made a great impression on her, as I often seemed to do with the ladies. But I was suddenly very glad I'd behaved the way I did.

At Bondi Junction I met up with Rich again and in a car heavily loaded down with paintings we headed back up the Pacific Highway, over the bridge, up past the Ku Ring Gai Chase and on to Newcastle. We changed drivers at fuel stops but otherwise carried straight on until we arrived at Coffs Harbour in late afternoon after driving for around nine hours. We found a motel and decided to break the journey by staying there for the night. Coffs looked like a fantastic place, and as the early evening sun began to set, I could see a dozen or more surfers in full, black wetsuits sitting astride their boards a hundred yards out, chatting to each other while patiently waiting for that elusive 'great wave'. The ocean had a wonderful blue-green hue as the huge waves rolled in slowly and evenly, breaking perfectly in masses of brilliant white bubbles on the enormous beach, then running back leaving sweeping ephemeral patterns on the wet sand. Gulls whooped and dived silently overhead, climbing higher as their outstretched wings caught the warm onshore breeze that swept in from the sea. My mind drifted and I thought how relatively close we were to Armidale on the map, but it was sadly impossible to go there at that time. I vowed that as soon as I had a permanent address I'd write to Barbara and enquire as to her welfare.

Our final fuel stop was in Ballina, about 50 miles or 90 kilometres south of the Queensland border. A scruffy little man in oil-stained blue overalls emerged from an office in the petrol station and filled our tank for us.

"Where you goin' today then guys?"

"Brisbane," I replied, with some excitement in my voice despite feeling tired.

"You goin' up to Joe's country are ye?" he said, winking at us both. I hadn't a clue what he was talking about.

"Yiss we aaare…" Rich replied in his Kiwi accent, nodding. The man re-hung the fuel hose and leaned into the car.

"Good luck then fellas. That'll be thirty seven bucks…"

We set off again and I turned to Rich. "Joe's country? What the hell was he on about?" I said, brows furrowed and with a very quizzical look aimed straight at him.

"Joe Bjelke-Peterson, the Premier of Queensland. He's been there since the Stone Age and he runs the state like it's his own fucking country, the fascist bastard."

"Oh, right," I replied, still not fully understanding.

Rich and I seemed to have mainly opposite tastes. But one thing we did agree upon was the wonderful flat we looked at in Norman Street, East Brisbane. It was near the Wooloongabba cricket ground, *The Gabba*, but that wasn't the main attraction. We were offered a top floor flat, on the fourth floor, and it had a great view across the city centre from that part of Brisbane. There was a car park at the rear and it was a very clean and tidy two bedroom apartment. It was ideal. The bond was a whopping $400 but we moved in on the same day we arrived in the city. It was fully furnished and compared to the shithole at Warners Avenue it seemed like a millionaire's luxury penthouse.

Dave called round to the flat the first night we were there to see how we were settling in. Rich stated he had a headache so he wasn't very sociable. Dave asked me if I wanted to see the new office so I followed him down the stairs and out into the car park. His car was a Ford Fairmont, not an ordinary one, but a sleek, sporty version. It was dark blue with a beige vinyl roof and shallow twin air intakes on top of the bonnet. It looked beautiful and powerful, and certainly sounded as such when the growling 4.9 litre engine was fired up.

Once at the office near the centre of town I was given a tour of the rooms, all recently decorated with a smell of fresh paint and new carpets everywhere. This was soon destroyed when Dave pulled out the inevitable bag of cannabis and the two of us smoked while Dave set up a game of backgammon on his brand new desk. I hadn't played much before then and Dave showed me some quick moves which completely changed and speeded up the game. We played non-stop and each new game was more serious and focussed than the last as the smoking increased. Facial expressions became guarded and intense as though we were playing high stakes poker, and the short-cut moves across the board were made rapidly and without counting. A throw of ten would be split five ways and five pairs of two counters moved one space, then in another throw of the same number two counters were each moved five spaces, or one counter moved ten spaces and so on, often in the blink of an eye. There was an element of trust involved because sometimes you just couldn't possibly keep count, the game moved so swiftly across the board. Anyone watching us would have probably thought we were quite mad, as there was little conversation, and the games were played at astonishing speed, or so it seemed. Dave clearly thrived on winning and at that time was a much better player than I was. When I won my first game there was an immediate rematch at Dave's insistence in order for him to save face. It was a lot of fun and I enjoyed it. Later Dave took me back to the flat, driving across the city in his usual high speed manner and with calculated recklessness, with Jean-Michel Jarre music filling the car. It was actually a thrilling ride after playing backgammon and smoking for several hours.

The car that Rich and I were given between us was another

Ford Fairmont, but this time it was equipped with large black steel 'roo bars' on the front over the radiator grille and headlights, and a galvanised steel mesh grille completely covering the windscreen. We were going to be driving in the outer suburbs of Brisbane so these protective measures were apparently very necessary. The man at the car rental office told us, in a very informed kind of David Attenborough manner, that we would be unlikely to encounter any of the larger red kangaroos so near the coast, but a male eastern grey might easily weigh a hundred pounds or more, and so could obviously cause significant damage to vehicles. He didn't seem to show any signs of sympathy for the animals, and I wasn't even aware that different varieties and sizes of kangaroo existed. All the ironwork on the front made the car look and feel as though it had been made for one of the *Mad Max* movies or something that had been thrown together in a desperate hurry by *The A-Team*. It was a great lumbering heavy monster of a thing to drive, particularly when loaded down with paintings.

Within a few days of moving in Rich bought himself a very expensive Bang & Olufson hi-fi system. The sound this equipment made was just incredible, particularly after a smoke, even though our musical tastes were polar opposite. I generally listened to old stuff like Led Zeppelin and Pink Floyd while Rich listened to anything brand new and up to date. He and I lived our lives very close to one another, getting up at about the same time each day, usually mid-morning, and hanging around until mid-afternoon, when we drove to the office to report for work.

Once the paintings were collected we headed out of the city with our obligatory UBD (Urban Business Directory) road map of Brisbane and its suburbs. Business was good in the better aspirational outer suburbs of Brisbane. There were brick-built houses with nice cars and boats on the expansive driveways, owned by thrusting young professionals with lots of rooms in their new houses and no pictures on the walls. They wanted and needed some genuine Aussie scenes, original paintings to boast about to their friends, pictures they'd bought direct from the struggling artist who happened to call by the house one sunny afternoon. Yes it was all beginning to look up.

The first night Rich and I smoked cannabis in the flat we had a moderate bout of paranoia between us, and I wrote down our chances of survival in my diary. It consisted of a brief list of the positives and negatives:

The Negatives:
- Dave's gonna sack us
- Landlord's gonna kick us out
- Cops are gonna get us
- Not gonna sell any paintings.

The top two of the negatives were assessed after much debate as being completely unlikely and so these were awarded nil points each. The third was awarded half a point, and the fourth a quarter. So in total the negatives came to just 3/4 of one point.

The Positives:
- Nice flat
- Amazing hi-fi system
- Dave gave us $120
- Got some good dope
- Paid bond and first week's rent

The first four of these were awarded a whole point each, as they were all very definite and real. The fifth was only given half a point, for some unknown reason. The grand total of positives was therefore 4½, far out-weighing the negatives. So therefore based on these very precise and much debated calculations we both came to the conclusion that we were safe.

The first Sunday in the flat arrived and Rich stated he wanted to visit his brother who lived on the Gold Coast, just forty minutes' drive south of the city. His brother, he told me, would have some great dope we could buy. He would always have some dope, as much as we wanted and whenever we wanted it, apparently. There were a lot of varieties we could try too, and in many different forms. I didn't click at the time, but I later realised that this was because he was a dealer, and one of the best on the Gold Coast.

It was then that I realised for the first time that though it was on the east coast, Brisbane didn't have a proper beach of its own, unlike Sydney. It had a river, some mud flats, and Moreton Bay. Beaches with big waves were north or south at least half an hour's drive away in each direction. Not wanting to feel left out, Brisbane city later built a wonderful and permanent beach on the south bank of the river right in the city centre, though not actually *in* the river, complete with beautiful soft sand and real palm trees.

We pulled up outside a huge wooden house that was almost completely obscured from the street by overgrown trees and bushes. The exterior walls were in urgent need of a coat of paint, as it was peeling everywhere and the wood was starting to turn several strange shades of green in places. Inside was no better and the room we were led into was dark, gloomy, and heavy with the smell of latent tobacco and cannabis. I thought drug dealers were supposed to be very wealthy, so it occurred to me that he couldn't have been that good at his job.

Rich's brother, Pete, was a tall well-built man of solid stature, unlike Rich. Two other men were present in the room, sitting quietly in some enormous tatty armchairs and wearing faded denim clothing with metal studs all over, and big heavy boots. They had massive biceps bursting from the sleeves of their t-shirts and long straggly beards like members of the band *ZZ Top*. I hadn't noticed any motorbikes outside, but these two looked like a couple of *Hell's Angels*. After a twenty minute exchange of pleasantries during which I hardly said a word a clear plastic bag was handed over to Rich in return for $80. This apparently included some sort of wholesaler's friends and family discount.

"It's all Cairns heads, there's no leaf or bush in it, and it's fresh too, part of a new load that only came in yesterday. It's good stuff..." Pete said, as though needing to justify the high price. I took the bag from Rich and opened it up. The contents smelt incredibly strong, rich and sweet, and consisted almost entirely of 'buds', the top part of the plant where the THC was most concentrated. Pete threw in a bamboo bong, like the one I'd seen at Barbara's place, and Rich was handed a small wooden bowl.

"Here's the mull bowl, Rich. Give it a try…" Pete said, passing it over. It seemed it was customary to sample the goods prior to departure. I began to think that everyone in Australia had a cannabis habit, or was it just most of the people I was bumping into? Rich took out some small pieces of the cannabis and broke it apart in the bowl. Because he wasn't a cigarette smoker he didn't put any tobacco in the mixture, preferring it neat. He stuffed a cone tightly and lit it. He drew on the bong holding a cigarette lighter over the cone. The flame bent over at ninety degrees as it was sucked onto the mixture and was ignited. Rich drew in a long deep breath through the bong as though he was about to go pearl diving and held the smoke in his lungs. The bong was passed around the room and sampled by all.

After a few minutes I began to feel quite numb, almost as though the top of my head had been surgically and painlessly removed. My brain had left me, packed its bags and gone on holiday. The already dingy room began to feel dark and sinister; the two *Hell's Angels* seemed to be staring at me intently, not saying a word as Rich and his brother chatted away. I felt very uncomfortable. A second and then a third cone followed, and the bong eventually made its way around the room a dozen times. Suddenly I wanted to leave. I imagined myself standing up and walking towards the door and getting into the car, and I also imagined being safely back in the flat in Brisbane, or even back at Warners Avenue in Sydney, anywhere but there. I also thought that I might get my head kicked in at any moment by the two *Hell's Angels* characters, just for fun, and I could see my battered body lying on the floor in a pool of thick, red, congealed blood.

Then I heard a question clearly aimed directly at me from

across the room. It came from one of the *Hell's Angels*, and so I turned and glanced across at him through the smoky void.

"Where are *you* from then, mate?" a deep and very gruff voice said, with an emphasis on the 'you' part of the question. He was definitely talking to me, so I had to answer. What should I say, Sydney? Bondi? England? What if he hated English people, like I believed most Aussies seemed to?

"Sheffield, England," I heard myself say in what probably sounded very effeminate and feeble. I waited in the grim silence for the inevitable harsh ridicule and verbal Pommie-bashing that would follow, or possibly something much worse. Then the other *Hell's Angel* spoke up in an equally gruff voice and an extremely broad Queensland accent:

"Aww yeah? Oyd really loyke to go t'ingland eh?" and then the first one joined in again:

"Oy think oyve got some sort 'o' reladive in Pommieland eh? Oid sure like to go there too. What brings ye t'Oz then, mate?"

"Oh, sunshine, the beaches, the dope, you know, all the good stuff..." I could hear my pathetic voice but I couldn't quite believe what was coming out of my own mouth. There was a pregnant pause and then one of the *Hell's Angels* said:

"Aww yeah?" and looked directly at me just as he shuffled himself around in his chair. Was he about to get up and come over and land one on me? There was a further brief silence during which my fate seemed to hang on the edge of a dark smoky precipice. Then, to my surprise: "Well good on yer mate, nice one eh?" and everyone in the room started nodding in mutual agreement and appreciation.

"Have another cone, mate..." the other one said, reaching over and handing me the bong.

Everyone then began laughing uproariously. Suddenly something was incredibly funny, but I hadn't a clue what it was. I very nearly pissed myself I was laughing so much; in fact if I'm honest there may well have been a very tiny trickle in the underpants department at that moment.

BRISBANE

"In the Forest of No Vegemite"

I knew it was getting very close but I just kept stuffing the date to the back of my mind. A week away quickly turned into the day before. Then suddenly it was the morning of the day of my scheduled departure from Australia. Part of the conditions of acquiring a visa for Oz was possession of a return air ticket, and the day had now arrived. If I was to use the return half of my QANTAS ticket back to Athens I had to get down to Sydney somehow. I didn't get out of bed until ten o'clock that morning, so this was becoming increasingly unlikely. If I wasn't at Sydney airport by four o'clock that afternoon I'd miss the flight.

I dressed and as usual the first thing I did was light a cone, and then another. I wandered down the road to the café and ordered breakfast. I played on the huge space invaders machine as I normally did while waiting for my food. After breakfast I fed the machine with twenty-five cent coins and defended the galaxy from alien invaders for over an hour before returning to the flat. I felt incredibly conscious of the decision I'd already made. I knew I wasn't going back to Europe. I didn't want to go to Athens; what would I want to go there for? It was way too late now anyway.

At four o'clock I was with Rich in the car, cruising the western outer suburbs of Brisbane, on the fringes of the Australian outback in some wonderful Queensland sunshine. I gave it some quiet contemplation at the precise moment the aircraft would have left Australian soil, and I felt relieved and happy once the time had actually passed. The decision was irreversible, I was staying, and there was no turning back. I felt quite liberated. But now I knew that I had to live with the fact that I was an illegal immigrant. My six week tourist visa had also just expired.

I didn't *feel* any different as I walked the streets of Brisbane as an illegal immigrant. I didn't suddenly sprout long hairy antennae or nasty green tentacles. I didn't start robbing old ladies in the street and I didn't suddenly become a burden on the State. In fact nothing changed and nobody noticed at all. There were no immediate consequences of my change in status, but it did occur to me that perhaps I couldn't afford any kind of adverse encounter with the authorities such as the police in case they decided to check my status. But what was the worst that could happen anyway? Surely they would simply put me on the next available flight out of the country?

I'd heard some disturbing rumours of a requirement for foreigners to obtain a local Queensland Driving Licence if they wanted to drive on their roads, so one morning I ventured into Brisbane city centre on the bus to find out. I walked into the rather plush offices of The Queensland Transport Department in the wonderfully named Fortitude Valley and straight up to the enquiries desk. It turned out there was no legal requirement to obtain a local licence if not becoming a permanent resident. How long was I going to stay? I had no idea, but it could be a long time now that my ticket had gone. Perhaps I should obtain one anyway? I filled in some quite vague background paperwork and luckily I was not asked to produce my passport or otherwise show right of abode in the country. I then took a very basic written road traffic examination and with the appropriate payment I attached a copy of my full UK driving licence. After a short wait I was handed a crisp new Queensland Driving Licence printed on sky blue card. From that moment on this document would become my default ID if challenged by any of the authorities. It was a safe and sufficient form of identification without anyone seeing my passport or calling into question my immigration status. One look inside my passport at the expired Australian visa and that would inevitably be game over.

Dave was expanding the business and recruiting more

young people to trudge the streets and make money for him selling paintings. A rather self-confident chap arrived from New Zealand called Rob, and while in the office Dave suggested Rich and I should accommodate him in our flat. So we took on this stranger who was to sleep on our sofa for a while. He was a nice enough bloke, easy-going, pleasant, and he seemed to be good at selling paintings. Because of this Dave liked him a lot. Dave liked anyone who was good at making money for him. Rob enjoyed taking part in the smoking sessions too and slotted into our way of life very quickly. One of the benefits of Dave expanding the business was the arrival of some young ladies to the team. Mary had only been working there for a week when she gave us all an open invitation to her house one Saturday night for a party. She was quite old actually, probably about thirty, but was confident, self-assured and she owned her own house. She didn't sell many paintings but this didn't seem to worry her too much.

It was a fancy dress event if anyone wanted to turn up dressed as such. I didn't bother with a costume but Rich emerged from his room wearing a skin-tight, fluorescent lime green, one-piece bathing costume, similar to the yellow one-piece worn by Sacha Baron Cohen's *Borat* character. This was before *Borat* was created and Rich just looked absurd. Rob and I gazed in open-mouthed astonishment at him standing in the kitchen while he made himself a cup of tea before we left. His lumpy crotch area was huge and his outfit was drawn tightly like cling-film over his bulging genitalia. You know those weirdly embarrassing moments when you don't want to look, but you do anyway? The rim of Rich's helmet could clearly be seen boldly pressing up against the inside of the stretchy Lycra. Why on earth was he wearing such a thing? Who was he trying to impress? He'd never pull a bird looking like that, or would he? Granted that it took a huge amount of courage to wear such a revealing piece of clothing in public, and I actually admired him for this, for the courage, that is, not the clothing, but really!

Mary's house was quite a distance away in the outer

suburbs and was a typical wooden Queenslander built on stilts with a garage and workshop underneath. The back garden was colossal, probably an acre or more, and was huge by British standards. In the kitchen there was all manner of alcohol available, and the three of us placed our meagre offerings of a few tins of Tooheys beer on the work surface. Most people were outside the house in the back garden because it was a very warm night, so Rich took off his jacket as he walked down the back steps, revealing his leotard like Joan Collins peeling away her fur coat at the Oscars. There were some sharp intakes of breath and a few sniggers, but Rich took it all in his stride. He didn't seem bothered.

I saw Dave sitting at one of three long wooden tables on the back lawn, chatting away to someone, and when he looked around he indicated for me to join him. He'd clearly been there for a while as he seemed to be making himself completely at home.

"Wanna smoke?" Dave said to me, which was almost always the first thing Dave ever said to me anyway, wherever we were, and all the time. But this was different. He smiled when he pointed at the numerous ornaments on all the tables. Placed at intervals of every couple of feet was a huge wooden mull bowl the size of a large fruit dish, and each one was piled high with dried cannabis leaf. Dotted all across each table were perhaps half a dozen bongs, most of which were standing unattended but with wisps of smoke drifting up from them, having clearly just been used.

Dave passed me the nearest bong after stacking the cone with dope from a mull bowl. Even in the half-light of the garden I noticed Dave's eyes were badly bloodshot, as though he'd over-indulged already. He was completely off his face and looked like a smiling Dracula, and it was clear he was trying his unsuccessful best to hold it together. I'd never seen so much cannabis. People walked up and sat down briefly, grabbed a bong and took in some smoke before disappearing away again. There didn't seem to be much alcohol being consumed, and despite the fact the party was well attended, the atmosphere was all very serene and civilized.

We stayed the night at Mary's, as did quite a few other people. Bodies were draped across every bit of soft furniture and filled the floors in every room. Some people clearly thought they might help out with the limited floor space available by lying on top of someone else, which I thought was quite admirable of them, though they didn't look like they were doing much sleeping. No-one was capable of walking, let alone driving a car. I certainly didn't want to risk driving in the condition I was in. I'd driven a car once before when badly stoned and had drifted past a red light at a main intersection in Brisbane city with perfect accidental timing as though I was in an old *Buster Keaton* movie, missing opposing vehicles by a few inches. I decided after that near-miss that driving while completely off your tits on weed was not actually a sensible thing to do. Not for the first time I thought my guardian angel must have been on my shoulders on that occasion.

A few days later the party was discussed in the office, along with Rich's outrageous outfit. Dave revealed that Rich was gay. Didn't I know? The truth is, even after living with him for weeks I hadn't guessed. Maybe it was just that it wasn't my concern? But I had entertained a couple of ladies from work, one of whom was Dave's sister Eileen, when Rich remained forever single. Maybe he didn't feel inclined to bring anyone back to the flat? Or was it that he had just not met anyone? Suddenly a few things fell into place, and in particular the shocking lime green leotard at the party. But I still wasn't bothered, and it certainly didn't bother me in the least that I'd been sharing a flat with a gay man. Why should it? In fact, if anything, I was a little concerned at Rich's obvious reticence in not coming forward about it. What did it matter?

THE CASTLE OF THC

Chapter One

One day in the Forest of no Vegemite, there lived a beautiful princess, and she lived all alone. Her whole life was a total catastrophe, nothing ever going right at all really, so she decided to go and do something about it. She went to get something from the shops with 4/6d with her, and decided to go and go again so she really increased her lifespan by becoming a 'go-go' dancer because go-go dancers were well paid individuals at the present time of life we are concerned about right now. I'm not really interested in writing any more of this trite shyte so I'm signing off now so you can tell your teachers to go and stuff their so-called do goody goody and you'll be goody goody after how many years of practicing.

We continued our weekly routine of driving down to the Gold Coast every Sunday to collect our bag of cannabis, but now because Rob was with us the bag had to increase in size from \$80 to \$120. When the huge water park opened up after the winter closure we spent a wonderful afternoon on the waterslides smashed off our faces splashing about and giggling like little kids on all the fantastic slides. Winter in Brisbane had not been the winter I knew in England. The coldest it ever fell to in the day time was around seventeen degrees Celsius, or the low sixties Fahrenheit. The tropic of Capricorn was only a couple of hundred miles up the road at Rockhampton, so it really was a sub-tropical city. Even though I still didn't wish to return to the freezing grey winter days in England, very occasionally I fancied there might be a cold frosty morning, just once, to break the monotony of hot weather. This was more keenly felt as spring turned to summer and the temperatures really began to rise. The humidity was something I wasn't used to. In the deserts of the Middle East the air tends to be hot and dry, but here it was entirely different. After a refreshing shower, the mere act of drying yourself afterwards would cause a lathering sweat, almost making the first shower seem quite pointless.

Chapter Two

Basically though, the princess looked around for some means of improving her general outlook on life by improving her standard of living, then maybe her success rate would climb. She sat and pondered and wondered and squandered, but she could not find a suitable solution. She got up and turned the record over and the melodies chimed in her ears like distant church bells and she realised she was out of it again. She rang the bell for the servants and in walked a strange-looking guy with distant eyes, and handed over a plastic bag full of herb-smelling new mown hay and she knew then where the answer lay. The castle was so large, with no fire, in winter it was pretty cool, but she had a tube she could look at now and again, a drinks maker, coffee, tea, water, milk, and food maker combined, though the latter became very unreliable as sometimes it produced nothing; with understandable and straighteningly disastrous results when the princess was munched by her castle's very brick and mortar. Yes, the answer appeared out of the sound waves, a picture formed, words drifted and swayed into her ears and onto her brain, and finally Fantasy Island came into view. She knew it was the end...

On one of our visits to Rich's brother he supplied us with cannabis resin, also known as hashish, which was very popular in the Middle East. Our first piece was a brown lump tightly wrapped in cellophane about the size of a man's thumb and cost an absolute fortune. Rich said it was worth the money and preferred it because you could inhale the smoke from it without adding any tobacco. Using the cooker hob, a flat knife was placed on a hot ring and heated for a few minutes. Then a few crumbs of the stuff were placed onto the knife and it started to burn, emitting tiny thin wisps of smoke as it did so. Then using a small tube, ideally a biro, you sucked up the smoke directly from the knife. It worked very well, and was clearly a healthier option to smoking tons of the hot plant leaf with tobacco. We tried another variant on the same thing, this time liquid cannabis known as hash oil. It came in a small glass phial and was spotted in tiny drops onto an ordinary cigarette whilst it is smoked. I didn't notice any real difference in the effect, but it was a lot more expensive.

Far away, on the other side of the world, England and my home were still there, or so I assumed. I didn't give any of it much thought at all. I felt quite detached from it, as well as from everything else, and my Englishness was beginning to fade as though it was being bleached away on a daily basis by the strong Australian sun, like newsprint on a bright windowsill.

Chapter Three

The princess was killed by too many distractions. She was reincarnated as an ordinary guy living on vegetation-conscious Earth, a rare planet unfortunately not yet succumbed to rampant Mortifierism. Mr Jones taught the art, and I fell into a huge vat of custard. So what? When custard de de der derr is as ooh! Costly as this, the space mysterionic invaders must be saved, before too much too late and almost cap-less and shampooed. She said "No!" so she got up and had a game of delicious cardz...

I wrote very few letters home to my parents but many more to the friends I'd left behind. I did feel quite isolated living in Australia, being so far from Europe and everything I knew. I wrote to Sean frequently. Sean had become one of my best friends I'd made while travelling. I met him in Germany the year before and we'd met again on the kibbutz in the Negev Desert in Israel. Along with Pat and Paul the four of us had bought brand new bicycles in Germany and transported them to the kibbutz from where we had planned to ride them all the way through Africa to Cape Town. This was an exciting but completely unrealistic idea that no doubt had developed very late one night in a haze of German beer and wonderful naivety. Four Israeli families on the kibbutz were delighted with their purchases of brand new German bikes, this being one of the better legacies of quite a mad summer I'd spent labouring in all weathers in Schleswig-Holstein, north of Hamburg.

Sean had since returned to his home in Dublin but was also now seeing Anika, the girl from Amsterdam. I had a letter from Sean stating he was now in Holland with Anika and that they were very interested to hear about my experiences in Australia. I wrote back with great enthusiasm, telling them how easy it was to make huge sums of money selling Dave's paintings. Usually these letters were written when I'd been smoking and so they were very often quite detached from reality and wildly exaggerated. But Sean had a great command of the English language and could be very talkative and energetic at times. I really thought he might make a great salesman, so I repeatedly encouraged him to come over. I also wrote letters to Jane, the English girl I'd left behind at the kibbutz six months before. I didn't really miss her very much, and sadly I didn't have the courage to tell her this. Consequently, and to my surprise, Jane announced she was travelling to Australia very soon to see me. I could easily have told her not to bother but I just didn't.

Jane arrived in Brisbane and must have sensed a cooling

in our relationship. But with despicable selfishness I exploited the situation and she moved into the flat immediately. Rob also entertained ladies in the flat and facing what was probably a very uncomfortable not to say a crowded situation, Rich decided to leave. He left Brisbane altogether and returned to Sydney. They say you only miss what you no longer have. I was sorry to see Rich leave on that very hot and sticky Brisbane afternoon. We'd been through a lot and had lived together in quite intimate circumstances for a long time. Now he was gone. Rich said a curious thing to me when he left:

"Have a nice life" which I found a strange thing to say, and very final. We'd meet again, surely? Sadly I never actually saw him or even heard from him again.

Life in the flat at Norman Street developed quite a routine, if you could call it a routine. Waking up in the morning and having a few cones almost straight away and getting stoned even before getting out of bed properly, then playing on the space invaders machine down the road for most of the day, until work from six o'clock until nine o'clock in the evening selling paintings. After work I'd return to the flat and get stoned again, staying up until four or five o'clock in the morning every morning writing, reading, listening to music or just watching television. More often than not it would be the television that occupied me due to the fact that I was just too stoned and too tired to concentrate on anything else.

I was enthralled by re-runs of *Fantasy Island* starring Ricardo Montalban and I even found the adverts mesmerising, including those that were clearly designed to stir up some sort of affection for the city in which we were living. Every now and then there would be cheery civic jingles played by the TV networks that became almost permanent ear worms in the brain, such as: 'Love you Brisbane, from the mountains to the sea...' usually set to some sickly sweet anthemic tune. For a while I actually thought these *were* Australia's National Anthems, they were played so often. I just couldn't imagine anything like this happening in the UK in-between programmes or perhaps before tuning in to the nightly edition of *Look North* broadcast from Leeds. There would be a sudden light-hearted jingle blurting out from the TV: 'Love you Yorkshire, from the moors down to the sea...' just before the dreary female presenter looking as plain as an old boot would sit wincing at her grim-faced male sidekick forcing a smile at the camera. It just wouldn't happen.

I wrote some poetry in the rare moments when I was lucid enough, but once the THC kicked in I'd write nonsensical rubbish such as '*The Castle of THC*' and so on. Why did I keep writing about a princess stuck in a castle? What the hell was that all about? I thought such writing was wonderful when I wrote it of course, but in the cold light of day it was clearly complete crap. There were quite a few senseless scribblings like that, and three chapters survived only because they were in amongst the text of my diary, otherwise they too would have been put where they belonged, in the bin. But they were a reflection of what was happening to me at the time, and that's why they are included in my story. I was destroying myself and burning myself out and I just couldn't see it yet.

I missed the ocean and tried to make as many trips to the Gold Coast as possible. Yet more Kiwis arrived in Brisbane to work for Dave, friends of Rob's that he'd invited over. I drove to the airport to pick one of them up. Karl was tall and wiry with thick, shoulder-length hair and seemed a really nice chap. I drove the Ford Fairmont back to East Brisbane the same way Dave drove his car, weaving in and out of traffic like an idiot. Karl was impressed but I was just very lucky I didn't attract the attention of any cops or have a smash.

The first weekend Karl was living in the flat I drove the four of us down to the Gold Coast. While showing off in a stupid and outrageous way, I drove the car at high speed on a wide road up a steep hill towards the sea, expecting the road to continue straight once we were over the blind brow of the hill. It didn't. Within a few yards of the top the road curved quite sharply to the left at sixty degrees, meaning there was nowhere for the car to go and no time to stop safely. The front of the vehicle hit the kerb extremely hard with an awful bang and some very loud scraping noises. It inevitably and immediately mounted the kerb and started to cross the grass towards a cliff edge. Luckily the car dug into the soft grass due to the fact that it had lost both of its front wheels, and so we came to a stop quite quickly. We were less than fifty yards from disaster. I felt incredibly embarrassed by this, and rightly so. I'd behaved like a dangerous idiot. For some strange reason I thought then that it would not have happened if Rich had still been with us.

One Saturday night a few people came back to our flat from the office and it was decided to throw an impromptu party. We had a full bottle of Jack Daniels and a heaped mull bowl full of strong cannabis. After Rich left, taking his wonderful hi-fi with him, Rob and I shared the cost of a relatively cheap but very loud stereo system. This was cranked up to number eleven and there was some dancing and general jigging about. The bourbon was all consumed, the dope was smoked, and everyone became very merry indeed.

No-one actually suggested we take off all our clothes; it was something that just happened, apparently quite spontaneously, as far as I can remember. I saw people rolling around on the floor doing things to each other and at about two o'clock in the morning while I and a couple of others were actually dancing about naked on the dining table, we heard some very loud banging on the door to the flat. It was initially ignored until it persisted and grew even louder. Someone turned off the stereo and Rob and I opened the door. I held a shirt over my otherwise naked groin area and was shocked and terrified to find two uniformed male Queensland police officers with guns on their belts standing there, looking extremely serious. I remembered what Rich had told me months before about the Premier of Queensland apparently running the place like a police state. I thought I was in serious trouble. I imagined I might be dragged outside and thrown in to the back of a police car and whisked away, never to be seen again. One of the cops couldn't hide a wry smile while the older of the two glanced inside and simply said to me:

"Keep the noise down, mate. There's been a complaint. Just keep it down okay? It's two o'clock in the morning." I suddenly realised how ridiculous I must have looked. Yet again I felt hugely embarrassed.

"Yeah, sure, no worries, sorry…" I replied. Luckily they didn't take the names of anyone in the flat, and simply turned around and walked away. The party was killed in an instant.

NORTH

"Where are you headed?"

I became aware of an incredibly strong urge to escape and for some radical changes to occur in my life. I also felt as though I should make a rapid reassessment of my relationships, particularly the one I had with cannabis. Who was in charge here, me or the drugs? It seemed I was becoming the servant to a very ruthless and unforgiving master. It may not have been physically addictive, but for me it was certainly habitually and socially addictive. For every task, in fact everything I did from wiping my arse to walking down the street I had to get bombed first. It was as though I had developed a real fear of sobriety and I spent virtually all of my time being detached from it. I knew I couldn't continue this crazy hedonistic lifestyle for much longer. I was beginning to wonder who the person was staring back at me in the mirror every morning. I felt unhealthy, paranoid, and more than a little claustrophobic.

I didn't know which was becoming worse, the irritating and persistent phlegmy cough I was developing or the increasing dominance of my THC-induced paranoia. An example of this was an occasion when Rich was still living in the flat. I bought two small plant pots and some growing compost and planted some cannabis seeds with great excitement and anticipation. But after nurturing them and watering them very carefully for weeks as soon as they appeared to germinate I became convinced the flat would be raided by the police so I disposed of them immediately. Not content with putting the tiny shoots in our own bin I dropped them in the main communal bin outside under cover of darkness and ran back into the flat. Even then it wasn't enough and I imagined they could be traced back to me somehow. So I got up in the middle of the night and retrieved them amongst all the filthy rubbish and ran for ten minutes down the road and shoved them deep inside a stranger's bin half a mile away, just in case. It obviously hadn't occurred to me that a stoned idiot running down the road at three o'clock in the morning clutching two cannabis plants might have aroused the interest of a passing police patrol.

Things were getting quite ridiculous and I knew I had to get away as soon as possible. I wanted to leave, to see more of the country, because apart from occasional visits to the outer suburbs I wasn't seeing anything of the real Australia. We'd once ventured about 60 miles west of Brisbane on a selling trip to a country town right on the edge of the wonderful Darling Downs called Toowoomba. It was quite hilly and I looked over at the tantalizing view further into Australia from the beautiful rolling hills and it fuelled my imagination for a greater adventure. I had to leave the stifling confines of the flat and escape, but where to?

I'd heard of pineapple picking in the Northern Territory where good money was apparently paid, and like so many such vague rumours acquired while travelling, it was believed without question. But how could I get all the way up to Darwin? It was literally thousands of miles from Brisbane. If I found work up there then I may decide to stay, possibly for years, or probably forever. I felt like hiding from the rest of the world, running away, because things just didn't seem to be going well for me in Brisbane any more.

I bought a small one-man nylon tent from a hardware store and a cheap imitation Swiss army knife to replace the one lost to security at Athens airport. I also bought a road map of Australia from a newsagent's shop which I brought back to the flat and spread out across the dining table. I'd done plenty of hitchhiking in Israel and France, so why couldn't I hitch around Australia? I was an accomplished hitchhiker and wasn't afraid to do it. But this would be very different to France and Israel. This was a huge country, with long stretches of desert and wilderness. But broken up into smaller segments it *must* be possible, so I decided I'd give it a try.

Even in some of the rare sober moments my idea seemed to make sense, and it began to evolve into something that vaguely resembled a plan. I'd set myself goals each day and head for specific towns a few hundred miles apart, and stop hitching as the sun set, if at all possible. I didn't fancy soliciting lifts from strangers in the dark, though I wouldn't rule it out completely. I already knew there were campsites everywhere in Australia, particularly on major roads, so I should be able to find places to pitch my tent, and for only a few dollars a night. If necessary I could camp by the road anywhere, provided I could find some facilities, mainly drinking water. It would be a real adventure, but it was also quite a daunting task, Australia was so enormous, a continent in fact and not just a country. But once I'd made the decision to go I felt suddenly liberated and I surprised myself at how determined I then became.

From my experiences of hitching elsewhere I knew that I had to get to the outer suburbs of Brisbane to catch a decent lift. It was no good hitching inside a city from one block to the next; this took up far too much time and was pointless. I was heading north so I needed an initial boost at the start if possible. I packed my meagre belongings which consisted of the tent, my thin green nylon sleeping bag, two changes of underwear, a second t-shirt, two spare pairs of socks, a towel, a diary and some pens. I also packed a pair of jeans, though I could hardly imagine ever wearing them it was so hot. I had a plastic one-litre Israeli army water bottle hanging from my belt, which I knew would be essential. I took my Walkman and half a dozen tapes. For my personal hygiene I had an aerosol deodorant that was almost empty, a new bar of soap, a razor, toothpaste and my toothbrush. I knew I could use the soap to wash my hair and also to hand wash my clothes. I was ready. I shoved it all into my faithful little A-frame canvas rucksack.

Rob, Karl and Jane drove me north past the Glasshouse Mountains and dropped me on the Sunshine Coast between Maloolaba and Maroochydore, about 60 miles or 100 kilometres north of Brisbane city centre. The three of them had decided to pay a visit to the area for the day and combine it with giving me my first lift. The Sunshine Coast was the area of northern beaches where Brisbane residents could find the sea, and is not to be confused with the Gold Coast, the wonderful beaches just south of Brisbane. It was a fine Wednesday morning in the middle of September, and it was very early, at seven-thirty. I hugged Jane and shook hands with Rob and Karl. Strangely enough between the three of them it was Karl that I was most sorry to leave. I'd developed a friendship with him and a rapport loosely based on a similar sense of humour.

I stood in my place on the edge of the tarmac as Rob turned the car around and they disappeared in the direction of the beaches. I wondered whether I'd see any of them again. I felt incredibly alone for the first time in months. But I never doubted that I was doing the right thing, even though I was literally trembling with a heady mixture of fear and excitement.

I stuck out my right thumb quite shyly at first at every passing vehicle that was heading north. There were quite a few in an almost constant stream of trucks and cars, and a large number of four-by-fours pulling trailers with boats on them, mainly very sleek and expensive speedboats, of varying sizes. They almost all headed off the main road towards the sea without stopping. Some of the drivers looked directly at me and pointed at the ground with their right index finger, signalling that they couldn't give me a lift because they were staying local. It was reassuring to at least get some acknowledgement like this now and again. After almost an hour a car pulled up and the driver shouted in my direction:

"Where are you headed?"

"North!" I shouted back.

"Jump in mate; you won't get far hitching from here, this road just goes up to Noosa. You need the Bruce Highway, I'm going to Nambour. You can get on it from there."

So without questioning him I ran up to the car and jumped into the front passenger seat for the first stranger lift of my adventure. The driver was a young man in his late twenties with gold-framed sunglasses and he repeated very apologetically that he was only going a short distance, and that it was better to head north from Nambour, where he was going, rather than the tourist areas of the Sunshine Coast.

"No-one will be heading north from there, mate, they're all locals and holidaymakers with their boats," and I nodded in agreement. I remembered all the speedboats on trailers that had been passing me by, full of bikini-clad girls and smiling, hopeful men about to have a wonderful time on the warm South Pacific Ocean. I thought of the day ahead and my own modest prospects by comparison and how the two couldn't have been further apart.

My first lift dropped me on the south eastern edge of Nambour, just past an enormous and very impressive fibre-glass pineapple the size of a house. I realised I'd been dropped off by Rob and the others in entirely the wrong place. It was a stroke of very good luck that my first lift had then taken me to Nambour.

"Just get to the other end of town and the road out leads back onto the Bruce Highway, okay? Good luck, mate!" and he turned off the road into the suburbs and was gone. I walked through the town on the main street to get to the northern edge. Nambour seemed a really nice place with wide streets lined with neat rows of shops. It was quite busy with the first of the day's traffic and the shops opening for business. There were signs for the Bruce Highway and so I stood at the edge of town near a large sheet metal road sign.

I didn't have to wait long before a battered Toyota pick-up pulled over. A scruffy old man wearing an equally tatty baseball cap who said he was a farmer took me on to a small town called Cooroy, which seemed to be little more than a fork in the road with some buildings around it. Then another old man picked me up within a few minutes in a very clean saloon car and took me all the way to Gympie, the next large town. From the centre of Gympie I walked towards the northern end of town, and started hitching directly outside a petrol station. This was quite deliberate on my part as it would give anyone driving off the forecourt a good opportunity to take a look at me and hopefully see that I wasn't an axe murderer. Not only this, close eye contact with the driver can help with the portrayal of a pleading expression, which can go some way to instilling a feeling of guilt or generosity, or both, in the driver and make them more likely to stop. I remembered this from my days of frequently hitchhiking in Israel, which was extremely popular in that country, particularly amongst soldiers. They would be quite aggressive in their hitching, stepping out into the road with their guns slung on their backs, bending over to look right inside the car at the driver, the way prostitutes do when soliciting. But it has a tendency to produce good results.

Quite soon my methods worked when a respectable couple in late middle age having barely got out of first gear stopped at the roadside to pick me up. They'd just emerged from the petrol station after filling their car with fuel. They took me all the way to Maryborough, over 50 miles or around 90 kilometres. I chatted to them about my travels and they told me they had a son about my age travelling around Europe at that moment. When we arrived at their destination, to my astonishment they took me in to their home and gave me a wonderful early lunch of chicken, salad, buttered bread and endless cups of sweet tea. "We would hope someone will do this for our son," they said to me as they kept filling my cup with tea. Their living room was plush, chintzy, very clean and tidy, and we drank from delicate fine bone china cups. I noticed from habit that they already had plenty of nice pictures on the walls, so they wouldn't have made good customers. Such kindness from total strangers was touching, and on my first day too! I explained at the end of the meal that the best hitching would be at the north end of town, so the man very kindly dropped me at the edge of Maryborough, and after wishing me luck, he turned the car around and drove back towards home.

It was in Maryborough that I noticed the humidity had increased greatly. The air seemed very sticky, adding to the stifling nature of the afternoon heat. I stood on the edge of town for over half an hour and I could see dark clouds gathering from three sides. It started to rain, but it was not cold in the least. It was a warm rain that had no cooling effect but quickly began to wet my clothes. I didn't have a coat or an umbrella, so if it continued I would need to find some shelter. Luckily, before I needed to, another couple this time in their thirties, picked me up and took me all the way to a town called Gin Gin via a larger place called Bundaberg, which by looking at the map seemed to be a long way round. But I didn't complain. I began to feel quite lucky, as I'd travelled a reasonable distance already and hadn't waited too long for each lift. It seemed I was doing well, and I was pleasantly surprised at my progress. This was until disaster struck.

MACKAY

"There are still some nice people in the world, eh?"

So far I hadn't waited any longer than an hour or so for a lift. Even an hour can seem a long time standing by the road in one spot staring into passing vehicles, particularly in the afternoon heat. But at Gin Gin after standing in the heat on the same area of tarmac for *four hours* I still hadn't any sign of a lift. From two o'clock in the afternoon until six, the drivers of every vehicle that passed simply ignored me. What was wrong with these people? I was fast becoming very hungry and my water bottle was almost empty.

The sun started to descend over the horizon and after a very rapid twilight it was dark. I didn't know what to do. Would anyone feel inclined to pick me up in the dark? It seemed unlikely considering they were not keen to do so even in daylight. Should I find somewhere to pitch the tent and stay the night? I was still contemplating what to do while absentmindedly throwing my right thumb out into the road. With another sudden stroke of good luck a car pulled over just ahead of where I was standing and began reversing back towards me. I ran up the road, pulled open the passenger door and leaned inside.

"I'm only going as far as Gladstone, is that okay?" the driver said, in a clipped Aussie accent, almost like that of a New Zealander. Gladstone! That was another 60 miles or 100 kilometres further north! That was excellent! I jumped in and couldn't believe my luck. Darryl was indeed a New Zealander, living and working in Gladstone, with connections to the rum industry, and he told me all about Bundaberg where Bundaberg Rum was made. He seemed very down to earth and I enjoyed his company. I was so relieved to be given a lift all the way up to Gladstone after the nightmare of Gin Gin. The road was quiet and we made good time, arriving in Gladstone at just after eight o'clock. Darryl actually found me a campsite and very kindly dropped me off at the gates before driving away.

The man in the office took five dollars from me and gave me a receipt. He pointed at the toilet block and seemed particularly proud to announce there were some new showers that had recently been fitted. I pitched my little tent for the first time on a dark patch of thick grass near some trees. I needed no persuasion to take a shower, and immediately after that I edged into my sleeping bag and zipped up the tent. It was the first time I'd slept in a tent since my days in the Air Cadets. I had completely forgotten how vulnerable you can feel with just a thin layer of material separating you from the night and the rest of the world. You can hear every sound nearby, the footsteps of people walking past and even some of their conversation. But it was my little home too, and it would be somewhere into which I could retreat any time I wanted.

I slept really well and woke up at seven o'clock the next morning lying on my back, very hungry, staring up at the pale orange sloping roof of the tent just above me gently fluttering in a light breeze. For an instant I had no idea where I was. Then as I gathered my thoughts I began to feel particularly refreshed and eager for the road. I had a good breakfast of eggs and sausages in the site café and I felt a strong and very welcome sensation of liberation as I packed my tent away and headed out onto the road. This was one of the biggest reasons why I was undertaking this adventure, to experience complete freedom, and it tasted absolutely wonderful. Things were going very well and it seemed I'd be able to cross Australia quite quickly at the rate I was going.

Gladstone was a few miles off the main highway so I needed a lift back there first, unless I could get one that was heading north at the same time. I started walking while thumbing with my right hand, hoping someone would stop for me. After twenty minutes a young man about my age pulled up astride a huge motorbike, the engine idling noisily next to me with a loud popping sound. The last time I'd been on a bike was several years before, clinging onto the back of a small Honda owned by a school friend, who rode it like a maniac around the streets of Sheffield. I didn't really enjoy the experience because I thought I was surely going to die with a broken neck in some rain-soaked gutter. I'd never owned a motorbike myself at that time and imagined I never would. They just seemed inherently dangerous machines, and I remembered a good friend from my first kibbutz days, John, was killed riding one near his home in Ilkley. I couldn't refuse a lift though, whatever mode of transport it was, so I put on the spare helmet I was given and climbed onto the back.

"Put yer arms around my waist or on the seat grip behind you, it's up to you, mate!" the man said, straightening the bike ready for take-off. "But just hold on tight okay?" I didn't feel inclined to put my arms around a total stranger, not on our first meeting anyway, so I reached my arms around behind me, crushing my rucksack a little in the process, and grabbed the steel grip at the back of the seat.

Using the analogy of an aircraft take-off was not an inaccurate description. The wide rear tyre of the bike spun ferociously and threw up bits of gravel and dirt in a great filthy cloud of debris, and once it touched firm tarmac the acceleration took my breath away. In seconds we seemed to be travelling at a hundred miles an hour or more, and in a few minutes we were passing cars and trucks and leaning into bends like we were veterans of the Isle of Man TT. We were both wearing little more than shorts and a t-shirt, so I pushed to the back of my mind any thoughts of what might have happened if the bike had lost grip and we made sudden bodily contact with the road. There's no doubt I found the experience totally exhilarating, but at any moment it could have easily been the very last thing I'd experience too. Within minutes we'd reached the Bruce Highway and the bike stopped at the junction. I tapped the man hard on the right shoulder.

"Thanks, mate, I'll get off here!" I shouted, making very

sure that I was heard and understood. The man insisted he could take me all the way to the next town, Rockhampton, 60 miles or 100 kilometres further on, but I politely declined, even though we'd probably be there in about twenty minutes flat. The rider initially seemed a little disappointed with my decision but then appeared quite unconcerned and secured the spare helmet to the back of the seat. He turned around and found a gap in the traffic and with a loud roar from the engine he sped away.

I stood by the road in agony. I'd been gripping the hand rail behind me so tightly all the joints in my fingers hurt. My neck was painful and my arms were also giving me some excruciating pain. I took a swig of water from my water bottle and rolled my head around on my shoulders and then flung my arms about wildly like a mad windmill. I must have looked quite odd to people driving past. The pain quickly subsided and I began sticking my thumb out into the road again.

A flat-back van pulled up. The driver just shouted: "Jump in the back!" so I climbed over the back and rolled onto the floor among some large sacks and rough planks of wood. It was a great way to travel on a hot day. It also meant that I wasn't obliged to make conversation with the driver, which sometimes was a bit of a chore. At a more modest pace but much safer, about an hour later the van pulled into Rockhampton. If I had a camera with me I would have taken a photograph of myself standing at the monument to the Tropic of Capricorn, which runs straight through the town. As though to emphasise this geographical fact, it became particularly hot and uncomfortable as the morning went on. I was now about halfway up the Queensland coast between Brisbane and Townsville.

I walked to the edge of town in the stifling heat and began hitching. It was to become my worst day of the trip so far. Just after ten o'clock that morning I started hitching to get out of Rockhampton, and I was still standing in the same spot in the road all through the midday heat right up until four o'clock in the afternoon. I stood in the baking heat for *six hours* with no luck whatsoever. It seemed the four hours I'd spent standing in Gin Gin was only the start, a mere taster of what was to come. Hitchhiking across Australia was suddenly not as easy as I'd first thought. Vehicles were passing but no-one wanted to stop. Maybe it was the sheer distance involved? It was over 250 miles or 400 kilometres to the next town, Mackay.

I was utterly exhausted and decided to call it a day, so I wandered back towards Rockhampton and found a campsite. I paid $7 for a pitch and for this I enjoyed a long and wonderfully refreshing shower and some excellent facilities. I had neck ache and back ache from standing still for so long and after my shower I had a lie down on the grass for a while and almost fell asleep. I checked myself because I needed to do a few chores before dark.

I pitched the tent and washed a few clothes by hand in a sink and hung them on a line to dry. I then found a café nearby selling wonderful fish and chips, so I tucked into a large portion, washed down with a litre of milk. I also bought some buttered bread rolls for morning. As the sun set I climbed into my tent and very quickly fell asleep.

I slept really well and woke before dawn. I ate my rolls and packed my tent away. I stood by the road very early at six thirty. It was a beautiful fresh morning and I was quite optimistic despite the events of the day before. I felt as though I should stretch the day to widen my chances of getting a good lift, I was so fearful of standing there for another entire day with no luck. I was rewarded when after only fifteen minutes a bright yellow customized VW Beetle pulled up next to me. The driver was a young woman probably a year or two older than me.

"Where are you going?" she said, smiling at me from the car.

"North, Townsville." I replied.

"I'm going to Mackay. Wanna lift?"

"Sure!" I shouted back excitedly as I opened the passenger door and climbed in. Kathy was a trainee nurse. She had long curly red hair, a round pretty face, pale blue eyes and freckles.

Her bottom lip was badly blistered from sunburn, and she remarked on it straight away, as though apologising for it, commenting how painful it was.

"No-one's going to give you a lift from here. It's too far," she said, glancing at me as we set off.

"You have," I said in reply.

"Well, yes, but you're lucky, very lucky."

We talked and joked together, and I told her about the motorbike ride and the old couple who took me in and fed me.

"There are still some nice people in the world, eh?" she said, smiling. After initial introductions and brief life stories during which I told her I was from Sheffield, to my astonishment she informed me that in two years' time she would be starting a placement at a hospital in England, in Chesterfield. This was only twenty minutes' drive from Sheffield.

"What about family here in Australia, and…" I hesitated for a moment before I carried on, "your boyfriend?"

"Aww, there's no worries about that. I'm well and truly single at the moment anyway, but you never know eh?" she smiled at me and I noticed the freckles on her arms extended down onto the backs of her hands, which were small and delicate. Her hair was continually blown around in the hot breeze from the open window next to her and in profile she looked very feminine. On the initial meeting and eventually after being in the car together for over three hours I felt quite drawn to Kathy. She seemed to be a lovely person and was very pretty. She told me which department she was due to specialise in at the Derbyshire hospital and told me to look her up if and when I finally went home.

When we arrived in Mackay I didn't want to get out of the car. I wanted to stay, possibly find some work in the town, maybe see Kathy again later that night, or the next day? I wanted to get to know her better, but I didn't have the necessary confidence to make any direct suggestions. It's the strangest thing in life to wonder what would have happened, and what *could* have happened, if only we'd been brave enough to have made some slightly different decisions. It's easy to say in hindsight, and I failed miserably, but if you see a chance and it feels right at the time then don't hesitate, just take it. You spend a very long time in that box underground.

Kathy dropped me in the centre of town and we waved at one another as she drove away and the yellow Beetle eventually disappeared around a corner.

TOWNSVILLE

"I'm on my way to Darwin, hitching..."

I walked several miles to the edge of Mackay. It was very hot but by now I was getting used to being wet with sweat all over my body, all the time. A man pulled up and offered me a lift about ten miles north so I took it. It could have been a mistake because I was then dropped in the middle of nowhere in a place that was probably too small to even have a name of its own. But there was a pub of course, and it looked very tempting. As I stood near the front of the pub with my thumb out, a car pulled up and a man in his early twenties jumped out.

"Thanks for the lift!" I heard him shout to the driver as the car then sped away. He was clearly a fellow hitchhiker. He stood by the road about twenty yards away from me, a large red rucksack at his feet. I noticed there was a Canadian maple leaf flag sewn onto the top of his bag. The occasional vehicle passed and we both stuck out our thumbs to no avail. I was irritated by the fact this man wasn't playing by the rules. The person who was there first should get priority over the lifts. This second person should therefore be standing *behind* me, so that I stood a better chance of getting the first lift. That was how it worked. The man seemed oblivious to this though, and my irritation with him poisoned my attitude and prevented me from talking to him. In retrospect it may have been a good idea to get to know him. He was probably a nice chap, and I might have had a good time if I'd teamed up with him for a while. But it didn't happen. It was almost midday and it was becoming increasingly hot. Suddenly the first and only words this other man said directly to me were:

"Oh well, I'm for a beer, dammit!" and he picked up his

heavy pack, slung it onto his back and then walked into the pub. I was very tempted to follow but resumed some aggressive thumbing as soon as he disappeared, which was rewarded almost immediately when a large brown Fiat 131 *Mirafiori* came tearing past and juddered to a stop in a huge cloud of dust fifty yards ahead. I ran up to the car and spoke to the driver. I always tried to have a quick chat if I could, before climbing in. This was not only to find out where the driver was going, but also in an effort to make an instantaneous judgement as to what type of person they were. I started doing this before I accepted most lifts, and I *never* threw my bag into the car ahead of me, just in case. I wasn't carrying the Crown Jewels, but it was all I had, and I didn't want to lose any of it. I'd not yet had a dodgy lift, apart from the motorbike, and I wanted to keep it that way. Most of the roads I was travelling on seemed to pass through some remote areas, and so hitchhiking in these circumstances could potentially be quite dangerous. But it worked both ways. Kathy had certainly been very trusting or very naïve giving me a lift in her VW Beetle on the remote stretch of road between Rockhampton and Mackay.

The driver of the Fiat was heading for Townsville, so this was a superb lift. He looked like a business man of some sort and was about thirty, and he drove the car at high speed for almost all the journey. The car was a mess inside, with chocolate wrappers and miscellaneous bits of paper all over the floor and an ashtray in the middle of the dash just heaving with butts and overflowing onto the floor. Conversation was relaxed and easy and there didn't seem to be any pressure to keep talking. Anyway, once established into a lift, I usually began to relax with my drivers. I no longer felt the need to converse with the majority of them all the time, unless of course it was clear that they wanted to. Some of them did, because it may have been the main reason they picked up hitchhikers in the first place, but generally I learned there was no compunction to do so, and it could be tiring if you thought you had to make conversation throughout the entire journey.

After a few initial pleasantries the Fiat driver and I spoke mostly about the state of the road or the behaviour of other drivers. Then somewhere between Mackay and Townsville for several miles dense clouds of brown smoke covered the road and reduced visibility almost to zero. We saw the smoke in advance from miles away and so we were fully prepared when we reached it, but it was still a very strange and eerie experience driving through what looked like thick brown fog. It also felt a little like we were in a small aeroplane passing through cloud, because it wasn't always consistent, and cleared briefly at times before surrounding the car again.

"Bush fires," my driver commented, pointing over to the left whenever it cleared. There were long wide clouds of smoke rising high above tall orange flames that flickered and snaked across the fields covering hundreds of acres, apparently burning out of control and drifting across huge sections of the wide horizon. There were other fires visible too as we drove along, but they were far from the road. My driver told me they could have been controlled fires, crop burning, or accidental. Incredibly, they could even have been started maliciously by arsonists.

We drove through the towns of Bowen and Ayr, flying past without stopping until we eventually reached Townsville after four hours. I thanked my lift who then very kindly dropped me in the centre of town. I had no idea I'd just passed the Whitsunday Islands a few miles back, part of the Great Barrier Reef, and some of the best snorkelling in the world. This was not untypical of my travels; I'd been to Egypt several times but had never seen the pyramids. I seemed to collect world famous places that I'd been very close to and had *almost* seen.

I had an address to find in Townsville, some guys who had briefly tried the paintings business but had left after a few days having not had much success. 'We're moving up to Townsville, if you're ever up there, call in!' they said to me as they left Brisbane several months before. You should never say that to me if you don't really mean it.

I knocked on the door of the house in Wood Street, Munding Burra, Townsville, and even though it was late afternoon it was unbearably hot. I could never have imagined it would get hotter than Rockhampton, but it was. My clothes felt completely damp and heavy, and any physical exertion was incredibly tiring. The door was answered by Steve, one of the three lads I'd known in Brisbane.

"Hi Steve," I said before quite a long pause. There were no visible signs of recognition in Steve's face. "It's Jonathan, from Brizzy. How are ye?" I said, optimistically. Steve looked at me blankly, and then with some suspicion. He glanced into the street behind me, probably for a car, or someone else. Slowly some acknowledgement began to spread across his face. He smiled very slightly, but it appeared to be somewhat strained, just like the kind of weak, subtle smile that forms on a person's face while standing in the sea and taking a piss.

"Aw yeah? Jonathan, yeah! How are ye, mate? Come on in," and he ushered me inside the house. "What brings you all the way up heee?"

"I'm on my way to Darwin, hitching…" I replied.

"*Hitchhiking?*" Steve looked incredulous. "Is that how you got yerself heee?"

"Oh yeah, it's only taken a few days so far…" I replied, quite casually. I was led into the kitchen and offered a stool and then some coffee. Ten minutes later Brendan and Greg arrived, and looked as surprised as Steve had been to see me. They seemed astonished that I'd travelled the best part of a thousand miles, in a few days, and all at no cost to myself.

Initially I was made very welcome. I took a shower and changed my clothes. That evening we all sat around watching television. It was a Saturday and the day of the league final. I was given an ice cold can of Fosters in a polystyrene stubby holder, and it tasted brilliant. It was the first mind-altering thing I'd imbibed in days. The heat didn't seem to lessen as the evening went on and the huge, old ceiling fan in the lounge room whirred away loudly like an aircraft propeller, merely redistributing the hot moist air around every corner of the room.

The next day I washed some clothes in the sink with my soap and hung them out to dry. It didn't take long in the hot sun, despite the high humidity. On that Sunday afternoon everyone in the house went to an open-air rock concert in the town. It was apparently $20 each and I politely declined. They may have mistaken this for me being mean, but I had very little money and so to spend it on that would have probably been a mistake.

Later that night I wasn't offered any more beer. It didn't occur to me to buy any, or offer anything by way of a contribution. This, coupled with my boasting about being able to travel the country at other people's expense, seemed to cause some friction with my hosts. I didn't actually hear the exact words: 'Tight-arsed Pommie bastard' but I did hear something similar.

I woke up very early on Monday morning, before everyone else. I'd slept on the floor of the lounge room and was stuffing my belongings back into my rucksack, ready to make a quiet exit, when Greg walked into the room.

"Going? Come on, I'll give you a lift into town," he said to me, magnanimously.

At seven-thirty I was standing in Townsville at the beginning of the Flinders Highway into central Queensland, thumb out, ready to go. I noticed quite a few vehicles in front of me turning into the main road heading just where I wanted to go, but they were missing me. I walked about three miles in the early morning sun in order to get to the very western edge of the town. I then stood for over an hour until I was picked up but sadly only taken about ten miles further out of town. I did notice however, that there was more traffic in the main road, coming up from the south at a junction nearby, so it looked much more promising.

Nine o'clock passed, and still no lift. Ten o'clock passed, and I started drinking the water from my army bottle. I stood in the same little piece of road until midday when a truck finally pulled over and I climbed aboard. The driver was a farmer, driving home to Charters Towers, 75 miles into Queensland.

Charters Towers is the last major town before Mount Isa, which is the biggest and *only* large town in central Queensland, and has a base catering for The Royal Flying Doctor Service. This gives you a good indication of how remote the place is. It is 400 miles from Charters Towers, about 700 kilometres, and there's virtually nothing in-between the two places apart from a few very small towns dotted along the road. Anyone leaving Charters Towers heading west was therefore probably heading for The Isa, as Mount Isa was colloquially known.

I was conscious of the fact that this was probably where my real adventure might begin. The Flinders Highway takes you far away from the coast and all the tourist areas, and straight into the emptiness of the outback. You need a bloody good reason for travelling to The Isa because there isn't much there. It's a mining town and not famous as a tourist destination. I soon realised that vehicular traffic was therefore patchy and infrequent. In addition to this, who on earth would want to give a lift to a complete stranger in such circumstances?

I arrived in Charters Towers at two o'clock in the afternoon. I walked a few hundred yards in the increasingly dry dusty heat to the outer western fringes of the town, beyond all streets and buildings, so that I'd be the very last thing drivers would see as they ventured west. I stood on the low brow of a gentle slope and on a slight bend in the road looking back into the town for oncoming traffic. Gazing out in the other direction, west, I could see a vast expanse of desert-like wilderness. It wasn't rolling sand dunes in the classic sense, but quite featureless flat scrubland, as far as I could see. The earth by the road was sandy and very dry, and consequently however carefully I walked I couldn't help but throw up small cloudlets of yellow-red dust which left a fine powdery layer all over my boots. Every time large vehicles such as road trains thundered past they would leave behind in their wake a whirling mixture of choking dust and diesel fumes which parched my mouth and nose and made my thirst even more acute. The tropical moisture in the air seemed to be diminishing rapidly the further west I travelled away from the coast.

At around four o'clock I was still standing in the same spot. A late afternoon calm began to descend across Charters Towers and the gum trees near the road were standing inordinately still, with just the tiny top branches betraying slight movement on a very gentle breeze. I played mind games with my watch, allowing long periods of time to pass before trying to guess as accurately as I could just how much time had really passed. I became quite good at predicting the passage of an hour or even two hours.

My water was almost gone and I was considering having to retreat back into civilisation in order to replenish supplies, when I suddenly noticed a figure had just been dropped off on the edge of town a few hundred yards back. In order to comply with the unwritten rules of hitchhiking the new figure should have walked out of the town and past my position allowing me to be the first in line for any oncoming lifts. But this figure like so many others didn't seem to know the chivalry of the road, and just stuck out his thumb where he was. I was incensed by this behaviour and became obsessed with the treacherous newcomer never getting a lift. I could just make out that he was tall and slim with shoulder-length fair hair. He was really keen too, giving every passing vehicle the full thumb wagging routine while crouching down in the road to get a better look at the driver. I'd not seen this done by anyone else in Australia and I became very worried this chap could steal the one and only lift that might be heading that way all day.

Six o'clock came and then passed me by without anyone stopping. I was now getting seriously thirsty, but I dare not leave my position. I still hadn't been lucky, but then neither had the stranger further in the town. I was considering the merits of giving up for the day as the sun began sinking down closer to the western horizon. Just then a dark red Ute (short for 'utility vehicle', a car with a flat cargo area at the back) pulled up on the road verge in a cloud of dust right in front of the stranger on the edge of town. The hitchhiker threw his pack into the rear and climbed into the front with the driver. Damn it that was my lift!

THE ISA

"Scheisse! Das ist unmöglich!"

It should have been me climbing into that Ute! I was absolutely furious. It was unlikely that there would be another similar lift that day. As the vehicle approached me I prepared myself for the inevitable cheesy smiles and piss-taking looks from the occupants as they drove by, leaving me standing by the road. If that did happen then I decided I would probably head back into town and pitch for the night, very angry and disappointed and try again in the morning.

As the Ute drew nearer it appeared to wander around all over the road before I dared to notice that it had begun to slow down a little. Much to my surprise and relief the battered old Holden Ute then drew to a complete stop, pulling up immediately beside me. I threw a very optimistic glance at the driver, a corpulent thirty-ish white man with a rounded belly that looked like a hairy medicine ball protruding from underneath his much stained and very dirty dark blue t-shirt.

"Jump in mate, we've got room for another, eh?" he shouted at me, leaning over slightly and smothering the bottom half of the steering wheel with his belly. The front seat was deep and wide like an old leather bench and the first hitchhiker nudged his way closer to the driver allowing me room to get in. There was no back seat, so I did what the other chap had done; I threw my rucksack into the open back of the Ute, breaking one of my own golden rules by doing so. But this lift seemed somehow trustworthy, and he hadn't driven away with the other guy's bag. As soon as I jumped in and shut the door the driver set off, the vehicle rolling and weaving around clumsily over the edge of the road, throwing up huge clouds of dust before making firm contact with the tarmac.

"I'm Ron, how aaare ye?" the driver shouted, in a very broad Aussie drawl, "This is Herman!" Ron then said, indicating the other hitchhiker with his left hand, "We're headed for The Isa!" and I nodded in agreement and to confirm that I understood what he meant. I really wanted to be cross with Herman for almost stealing my lift, but Herman was smiling, laughing almost and it wasn't long before I realised why. The car was weaving around in the road in long gently elongated S-shapes from one side to the other while Ron was speaking. He didn't seem to think there was anything at all wrong with his driving. I smiled at Herman, who gave me a brief potted history of himself which included the fact that he was from Switzerland. I was about to ask how he came to be in the middle of Queensland hitchhiking, but my own story may have sounded equally strange so I didn't bother. Besides, with Ron's appalling driving it seemed we might not make it to anywhere else in one piece!

There were quite a few empty and some unopened beer cans strewn around on the floor of the Ute and which rolled around constantly. Sometimes one would get caught under the foot pedals adding to Ron's erratic driving and loud cursing. Every now and again Ron reached for a full can that was wedged between his very sweaty legs which looked like giant hairy sausages in his shorts, and take long gulps on it before shoving it back again. It was clear that he'd had quite a few already, and was still drinking heavily. It was then that I noticed just how much litter lined the roadside, as Ron promptly tossed another empty beer can out of the window to add to the rest. Cans and bottles were strewn all along the tarmac verge interspersed with other rubbish and the occasional mound of dead wildlife, most of which appeared to be kangaroos. The attrition rate of these poor animals on Australia's roads must be incredible.

Herman passed me a large floppy plastic bottle full of water, which I was very grateful for, even though it was warm and I had no idea as to its provenance, and then Ron shoved a packet of cigarettes in our faces so I took one, while Herman politely refused. I swallowed a few wonderful long gulps of water just before Ron aimed an enormous flame at my face that almost singed off both my eyebrows. He lit my cigarette and then his own, and we both began chuffing away while Herman who was presumably a non-smoker sat quietly between us. The windows were open wide but even so it couldn't have been very pleasant for him. Ron himself was also exuding a peculiar odour all his own, a mixture of very ripe body odour, stale cigarettes and bad beer breath. I know I wouldn't have smelt very rosy, but all these odours combined created a moderately toxic atmosphere in the cab of the Ute, particularly when someone added to the mix by farting.

Suddenly while in mid-conversation Ron leaned forward and threw his cigarette hand under his seat. He then started shouting for something, an animal, presumably, because he asked his passengers to look out for it. But what were we to look out for? I presumed it to be an animal, something that was apparently called 'Billy', because there were no other human beings in the vehicle, at least not in the front with us. Somewhere in the Ute was a dog, or so Ron claimed. Herman and I both shook our heads at Ron with some vaguely tragic expressions, but Ron kept on insisting his dog was indeed in the car with us. I imagined that perhaps at that very moment it was sitting all alone by the road, miles behind us, after the last time the door was opened, looking sad and forlorn in the calm twilight of Charters Towers.

Ron continued to shove his left hand blindly under his seat and into the front passenger foot well as far as he could reach, muttering something about a dog while trying to force his own head between his legs beyond his belly, at the same time attempting to keep his other hand on the wheel. The Ute weaved around in the road and the walls of the tyres screeched in protest as they dropped off the lip of the tarmac onto the dust and back on again. His lighted cigarette was in the same wandering hand and suddenly from under his seat there came an ear-shattering animal yelp as Ron pulled his hand out sharply from underneath him. His cigarette was now bent at the end having clearly just made contact with something living.

Ron gripped his cigarette in his teeth and then pushed his hand back under the seat. He pulled it out a second later having scooped up a tiny Chihuahua no bigger than a large rat which he placed on his lap after giving it a big wet slobbery kiss on the mouth. The poor little thing had a fresh black singe mark on its backside obviously from Ron's cigarette, and it had clearly been quite content to hide under the seat forever or at least until Ron had died.

"Say hello to the boys, Billy!" Ron said to the dog as it looked around the Ute in terror. Its eyes were wide and staring, as though it might die of fright at any moment. Ron was gripping it tightly around the chest as he held it onto his fat heaving belly, its tiny body quivering and trembling with nerves in the way little dogs do. As a gesture of affection or merely a symptom of its nervousness it then promptly pissed all down Ron's t-shirt and onto his shorts just as a very pleased but pained expression seemed to form across its face.

"You dirty little bastard, fuck off then!" Ron shouted, pulling it away from him quickly with his left hand. After all the apparent concern and affection he then tossed it down quite harshly onto the floor beside him as though it was a defective cricket ball. Herman and I just didn't know where to look. The little dog was then seen desperately scampering underneath the seats back into its favourite hiding place.

As true darkness descended Herman and I noticed Ron's head kept repeatedly dropping down onto his chest just as the Ute made some quite spectacular unplanned wanderings off the road and into the bush, missing several sturdy trees and clusters of rocks by a few feet on a couple of occasions. Clearly for our own safety the crew of the Ute had to mutiny, and soon. We suggested almost in unison to Ron that the three of us should share the driving. At first Ron was dead against the idea, but he was easily persuaded.

We pulled over and everyone moved along one place. Herman took the controls first and as the car started moving I heard him mutter some German which sounded as though it had come straight from *The Victor Book for Boys*: "Mein Gott in Himmell!" and then repeated loud utterances of "Scheisse! Das ist unmöglich!" The Ute meandered across the road from left to right in the same manner as when Ron had been driving, but Herman wasn't drunk. "This is not possible! You will see! You will see when you drive it, Ja!" he shouted at me, alternately laughing and repeating his German curses. Ron was by this time unconscious leaning his head against the nearside door, mouth wide open catching flies and dust and anything else that flew by the open window, and his poor little dog had been retrieved once again and was gripped tightly to his bobbling belly by his great shovel-like hands. We also had the very pungent smell of dog's piss which was another distinct whiff we could add to the rich blend of odours in the cab. Herman mumbled more Germanic curses when he told me the driver's seat was a little damp too, either from the dog or from Ron's sweaty backside, or both.

After a couple of hours Herman and I swapped over. It was then that I realised what Herman had been saying when he had first taken the controls of the Ute, and it wasn't anything to do with the seat being slightly damp. I was astonished to find that the Ute's steering had a delay on it of at least two full seconds or even more, so you actually had to anticipate where you wanted to go long before you needed to turn in that direction, hence all the weaving around in the road. My God indeed. How on earth was this happening, and how did Ron cope with this in an urban environment? It reminded me of one of the old physical aptitude tests for RAF pilot where you had a small steering wheel in front of you with which you had to follow a weaving pattern on a rotating drum that also had a similar delay on it. It was all about anticipation and alertness. It was good fun then, but not in the outback where you had to use the damned thing to avoid colliding head on with oncoming five hundred ton road trains. But just as Herman had eventually managed it, I was fine once I became used to just how much delay was needed and when. The nagging worry of course was whether the steering wheel might come off altogether. I didn't quite know what I would do then, maybe just hit the brakes and hope for the best. The engine didn't seem very healthy either, and was very unresponsive to the pressing of the accelerator pedal. There was plenty of fuel in the tank but this was dangerous country, and not somewhere you'd want to be stuck without plenty of water and in such an obviously unreliable vehicle.

Close to midnight some dark rounded lumps began appearing across the main highway, partially lit by the bright moonlight. At first I thought that I was probably hallucinating. I was getting tired and I wondered if I was having a THC flashback, if there was such a thing. Large, black, smooth-sided, solid-looking mounds lay dotted about on the tarmac ahead of us quite at random. Herman and I couldn't make out what they were at first; spread singly and in groups all along the road with many more of them lining the sides of the road. I was the driver on the first occasion this happened and we had to slow right down to get a better look and to ensure the Ute could safely negotiate the obstacles with the annoying delay in the steering.

Peering out into the narrow beam of the headlights ahead it became clear the closer we came to them that the huge lumps were in fact animals, buffalo or cattle, we couldn't decide which, with absolutely no road sense and clearly a long way from where they should be. If we'd struck one of these hefty beasts at sixty miles an hour there'd be absolutely nothing left of anyone, car or beast. They didn't seem interested in moving, as the apparently dead ones were a clear indication, and so any vehicle including a huge road train, would have serious problems encountering these things across the road. I couldn't believe this was happening and it therefore meant that from then on we just couldn't assume the road would be free of such obstacles, so our speed had to come down accordingly and alertness was forcibly increased. It made for an interesting and eventful drive.

When it was Herman's turn to drive again I opted to ride in the back of the Ute, in the open, in preference to snuggling up next to Ron and Billy. Ron was still fast asleep, and his very loud snoring produced some pretty vile odours from his cavernous mouth. Someone was repeatedly farting in quite an unrestrained manner too, and despite the windows still being wide open it wasn't possible to avoid catching the odd lungful now and again. A complete stranger's beer fart caught in the back of the throat has to be one of life's least pleasant sensations.

Moving outside into the rear of the Holden Ute was the best decision I could have made. I lay down on my back with my head against my rucksack and looked up. The hours that followed would become one of those very rare and utterly priceless travel memories and one of the greatest of my entire trip. As we streaked across remote central Queensland on the Flinders Highway the view suddenly snatched the breath from my lungs as though I'd fallen into an icy lake. In the spectacular midnight wilderness the stars of The Southern Cross amongst the other billions in the clear sky above seemed to touch the ground all around us. The dark desolation merged completely with the edge of the sky and everything in sight was bathed in a silvery ethereal glow from the moonlight. Looking on it seemed beautifully unreal, as though we were driving across the surface of Mars. Cutting our way through the vast featureless outback with our headlights reaching far ahead of us, I felt as though we ourselves were at altitude, tearing through space, the darkness forming behind us again in our wake as we moved. It was a truly unforgettable and magical experience.

At two o'clock in the morning Herman pulled up the Ute for a toilet break in a small settlement on the main highway called Julia Creek. It was probably just big enough to be called a town, and it consisted mainly of a few wooden buildings lining each side of the street for a few hundred yards. It had the general appearance of the town Walkabout Creek in the movie *Crocodile Dundee*. In actual fact the pub in the movie, The Walkabout Creek Hotel is real and is in a remote place quite close by called McKinley, about 60 miles or 100 kilometres south of Julia Creek.

At the time of our arrival it was understandably quiet, with no activity anywhere. It was decided we should try to get some sleep. I volunteered to disappear with my little tent and pitch it somewhere nearby, leaving Herman to sleep in the front seats of the Ute with Ron, or even in the flat back area as Ron was still snoring loudly, completely oblivious. I found a campsite a hundred yards down the road on the south eastern edge of town; I walked in quickly and quietly and pitched my tent as best I could in the moonlight.

In the morning I woke up just as the early dawn was streaking across the vast azure sky and I saw the countryside of central Queensland in daylight for the first time. It was impressive enough at night but this was simply extraordinary. The land around Julia Creek was flat. Just how flat can anyone ever describe a landscape that is flatter than absolutely flat? Not just *very* flat, like Norfolk, or Cambridgeshire, or the Fens, but *extremely* flat. It was so incredibly flat and empty that there was nothing to break the view as I stood gazing across the land into the far distance, literally as far as I could see. They say the Russian *Steppes* are similar to this: the distance just falls away along the curvature of the earth, uninterrupted, in a similar way to being at sea. It felt just like that, as though I was in the middle of a terrestrial sea, a vast ocean of land. I had never seen anything like it before and for a few moments it took my breath away.

The distances were so enormous, and the land so dangerous and inhospitable that it is no surprise that Australia's national airline was born from sheer necessity right there in central Queensland. The Queensland and Northern Territory Aerial Service, QANTAS, started life not far from Julia Creek in another small town a few miles south called Winton, with a single Avro 504 biplane in 1920. Crawling slowly along on the ground in the baking hot sun just had to be improved upon, even in those early days.

I de-pitched my tent and stepped back out onto the road. I found a café attached to the campsite and bought a wonderful breakfast of eggs, beans, and sausages. Then I smiled to myself as I remembered Ron, his dog and Herman, my other intrepid fellow traveller. I finished every scrap of my breakfast and as I stepped out into the street I lit a cigarette, the first of the day. There was no sign of the old Ute, and just as I was beginning to think they'd gone, the last building before the edge of town was a garage and there they were, having a puncture repaired on the Ute. Herman told me they'd set off earlier without me and developed a flat tyre which astonishingly Ron wanted to ignore, but on Herman's insistence they'd returned to fix. They'd also picked up another hitchhiker that morning too, an Aussie lad younger than all of us who Ron immediately nicknamed 'Sunshine'. He didn't seem very bright, or at least didn't give off much brightness, hence the nickname.

With the puncture repaired Ron and his little Chihuahua were fired up with renewed vigour for the remainder of the journey to Mount Isa, about another 100 miles or 160 kilometres across dusty and scorching emptiness. The sun was coming up quickly and it was clearly going to be another hot and cloudless day. Ron decided where everyone should sit in his remarkable transcontinental machine. Herman and I were to sit in first class, that is in the front with him and his dog, and Sunshine was to get 'out back' in the flat, open top area of the Ute. Suddenly Ron became distracted by the sad fact that there was apparently no more beer rolling around on the floor of the vehicle. After everyone had climbed in ready for a long trek he spun the Ute around and pulled up outside the only pub in Julia Creek.

We stood at the bar and started drinking beer despite the fact it was barely ten o'clock in the morning. Ron was enthusing to all present about what a good dog he had, which was a mistake because Billy then decided to show everyone just how good he was by shitting all over the floor of the pub in front of the bar. It was only Chihuahua shit, and so it was scarcely bigger than that of a rabbit, but it still looked and smelt very unpleasant. Billy then began to trail his lead, which was merely a rough length of string Ron had just tied around his neck, all across the floor. In an effort to grab it Ron stamped on the string and accidentally trod it into the shit and a puddle of piss that Billy had deposited moments earlier underneath Herman's stool. He lifted his foot when he saw the shit and the alarming sight of Billy half choking to death. Momentarily free from Ron's clutches Billy then tried to make a run for it. Ron chased him around the bar for several minutes shouting and cursing before he finally caught up with him as we all looked on in hysterics. It was great entertainment.

After three or four beers each the intrepid Ute set off again, with Ron at the controls, driving away from the safety of civilisation and into the arid wilderness. 'Sunshine', whose real name was apparently Keith, bounced around in the back of the open Ute completely exposed to the full sun, and we in the front were informed that if we misbehaved in any way we would join him.

We were now in a particularly remote part of Queensland and the roads were baking hot. Puddles and even huge lakes of imaginary water were everywhere, far ahead in the undulating road surface and all around us in the arid landscape that surrounding the road. These mirages looked so deep and real at times that when a vehicle approached in the distance it really did have the initial appearance of a tall ship cutting across a wide ocean.

After an hour we paused briefly in Cloncurry, a small settlement that was similar in every way to Julia Creek. I noticed my map had an interesting but unsurprising fact about this tiny place. It was where the highest temperature had ever been recorded in Australia, 53.1 degrees Celsius, or 127.5 degrees Fahrenheit, on 13th January 1889. It has most probably been beaten several times since then. On the western edge of Cloncurry the Ute picked up yet another hitchhiker, a young lad with a cowboy hat on his head. Ron therefore named him 'Cowboy' and said: "Throw him in the back with Sunshine..." as we set off again.

Luckily the Ute finally made it to Mount Isa when of course the first thing to do was to celebrate together in the pub. We bought each other a beer and then Ron was the first to leave, taking his dog and his Ute with him. He may have said where he was going but I have long since forgotten, and it's not mentioned in my diary. Sunshine then bought Herman and me a beer before he left too, then Cowboy and finally Herman. Our disparate little band of intrepid desert adventurers was no more. There are some rare occasions when you meet fellow travellers where it seems quite sad to see the end of the shared experience, and this was certainly one of them.

Not for the first time I found myself standing alone in a strange town with only strangers for company. It was there and at that moment in Mount Isa, one of the most remote places in Australia, when I suddenly thought of a song by *The Doors*, and the lyrics from 'People are strange'.

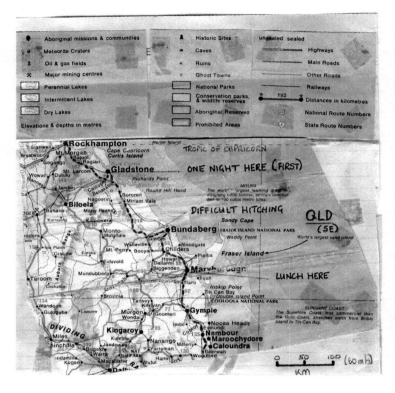

Stage one of my trans-continental hitchhike: Brisbane to Gladstone
– Part of the map I used and which has been taken from my diary

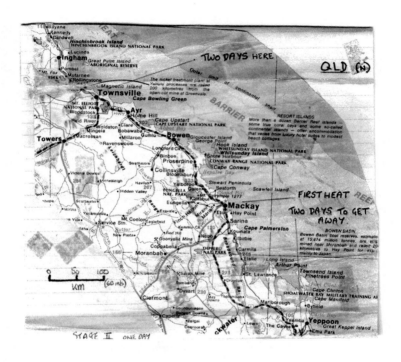

Mackay to Townsville

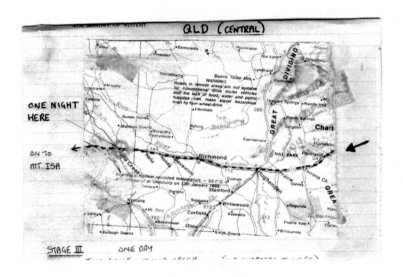

Charters Towers to Julia Creek

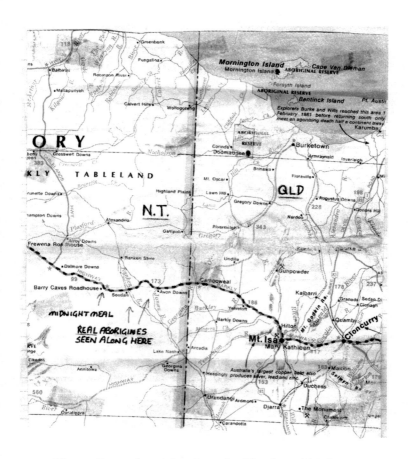

Mount Isa and crossing into the Northern Territory

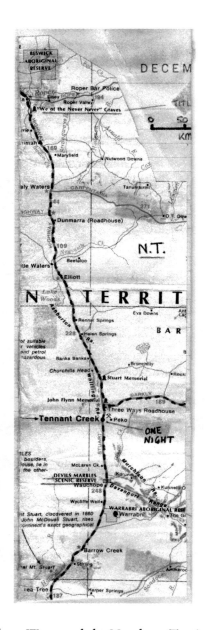

Three Ways and the Northern Territory

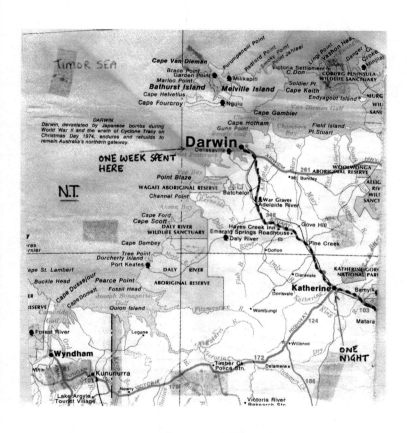

Destination: Darwin, capital of 'The Top End'

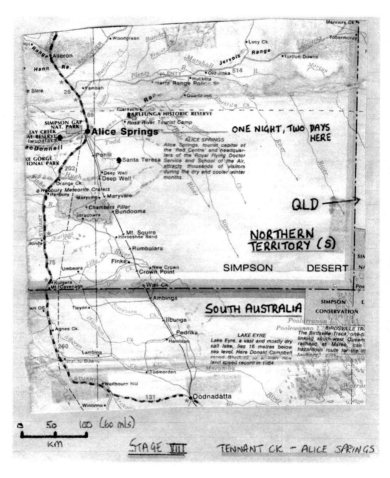

The 'Red Centre', Alice Springs & the Stuart Highway

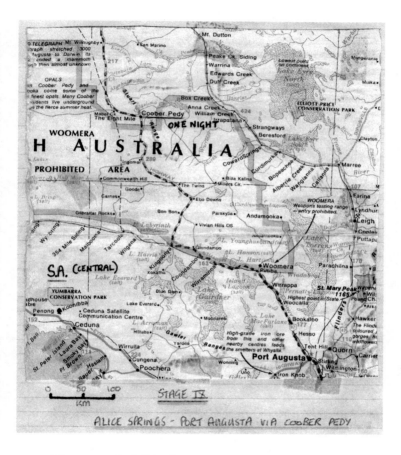

Woomera Prohibited Area, central South Australia

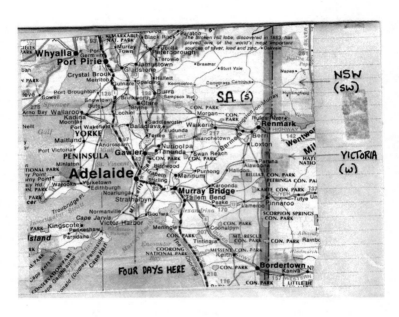

Adelaide, South Australia

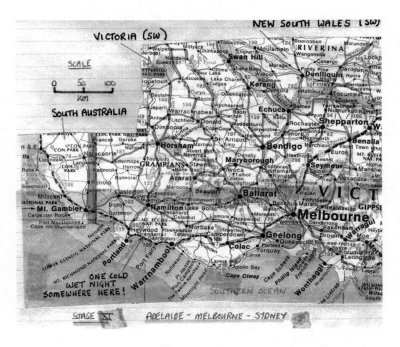

Melbourne, Victoria

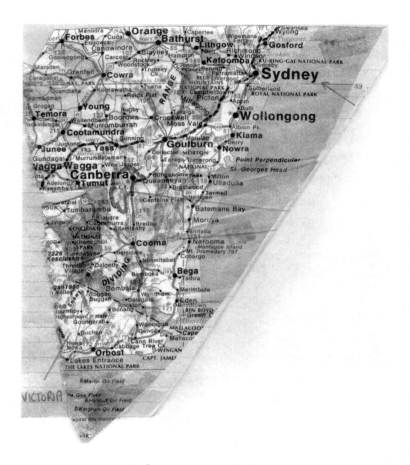

Sydney, New South Wales

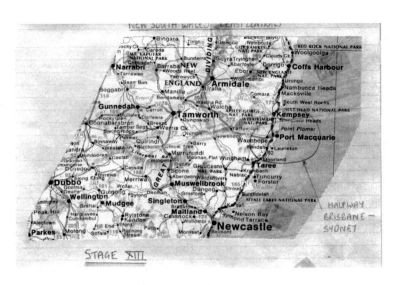

The east coast of New South Wales

Brisbane, Queensland, back to the start

Above: The iconic landmarks of Australia, Sydney Opera House and the Harbour Bridge

Below: The spectacular emptiness of the Australian outback

Above: The sign I made at the roadside in Mount Isa

Below: My tent in collapsed mode

Above: Some of The Devil's Marbles, Northern Territory

Below: The sad fate of many kangaroos

Above: The Stuart Highway in South Australia looking north

Below: The same road near the Northern Territory

Above: Coorparoo pool

Below: The house at Main Avenue, Coorparoo

Above L to R: Pat, self & Sean on the day of my Brisbane bank interview

Below: Brisbane's Story Bridge

Sipping Pina colada and still wearing my Doncaster Aero Club t-shirt before seeing in the New Year in Brisbane

Top: The house in Nicholson St, Greenslopes

Bottom: Dave's 4.9 litre Ford Fairmont

A Holden Ute, the ubiquitous transport of Australia

THREE WAYS

Barkly and Stuart

I finished my beer and picked up my rucksack. I had to get to the western side of town. My head was spinning a little as I stepped out into the bright sunlight. I felt good, and I also felt very optimistic. I'd made it all the way to Mount Isa fairly quickly without too many problems, so the next stage would surely be the same. I glanced around, half wishing they would be there, but there were no signs of Ron and his Ute, or Herman.

The next point on my map that I was to aim for was a T-junction, one of the biggest in the world, and probably visible from space. It was where the Barkly Highway through central Queensland joined the Stuart Highway which intersected it at right angles in a north-south direction and headed up to Darwin. The junction was called 'Three Ways', and there was nothing there but for a roadhouse. The nearest civilisation was Tennant Creek, a small settlement located a few miles south of the junction.

I started walking out of town, drawing great rolling arcs quite absentmindedly in the air with my right thumb beside me, and to my astonishment I was picked up almost immediately. Sadly I was only taken 3 miles out of town to the junction with the airport, where my lift was heading, and then I was abandoned. I looked ahead into the vast emptiness. It was beautiful but fearsome at the same time. Between Mount Isa and Three Ways there stretched a distance of almost 500 miles or 900 kilometres across the Barkly Tableland, and there were no towns of any sort in between.

The first thing I noticed about my chosen hitching spot was a fresh water tap by the road, just sticking out of the ground quite at random, like a stand pipe. I tried it immediately and it seemed okay. This was an incredible stroke of luck. The water appeared clean and clear, and was surprisingly cool, though initially warm in the first section of pipe above the ground. I didn't realise then just how much I would need it. I took out my Walkman and started listening to music. I still had a good beer buzz from the pub, and it was a beautiful warm sunny afternoon. In fact it was becoming quite hot.

Mid-afternoon became late afternoon, and I was still there. I played time games again with my watch and the hours passed by very slowly. There were vehicles heading in my direction, but none even so much as slowed down to take a look, never mind appear to have any room inside. I could see this was going to be very difficult. Whoever picked me up could feasibly have me in their vehicle with them for several days, and not just a few hours.

The sun dipped down below the outback horizon and quite quickly it was gone. I decided it was worse than useless to even attempt hitching from there in the dark, so I walked back into Mount Isa in search of a campsite. I pitched in the dark and was so exhausted I removed my boots as usual and went straight to sleep. Several hours later, deep into the night, I woke up feeling very uncomfortable. It wasn't because I was hungry or thirsty, or even hot. I was amazed to find that I was shivering with cold. I didn't have any really warm clothing with me but I put on my jeans for the first time and immersed myself as far down as I could into my thin nylon sleeping bag and zipped it up. I'd not experienced cold such as this for years. My tent was shaken around and blown almost horizontal in quite a strong cool wind, but luckily it held together, and it wasn't ripped to the ground.

I finally woke up at dawn, long before most other people, and decided to have a walk around the campsite. The wind had calmed but there were leaves and branches brought down from trees all across the paths and roads, testament to an eventful night. There was a small open-air pool, for the free use of campers, a café, toilets, and some excellent shower facilities. I changed back into my shorts and ate a pretty decent breakfast of eggs and bacon before packing my things away again in my rucksack ready to set off.

Up until that point, six hours was probably the longest I'd ever stood waiting for a lift, back at Charters Towers. I settled close to the tap again on the edge of town near the airport at ten o'clock that morning. I saw the marks around the tap and in the dusty verge that I'd made when standing there for hours the day before. The sun was already warm, and climbing up into another cloudless sky. Huge trucks passed but didn't stop or even slow down. Large heavily laden four-by-four vehicles trundled past too, but none of them stopped for me. There weren't any family saloon cars or smaller vehicles; the road was just too dangerous.

Midday arrived with the sun blazing down directly above my head. The effects of the bright light and heat were compounded by the fact that it was also reflected up into my face from the melting road. I thought how surprisingly tolerant of the heat I had become, standing there in full sun, without even a hat for shade. Without a doubt if I'd just stepped off a plane from England that day I wouldn't have lasted half an hour in those conditions.

I kept up the pressure, throwing my thumb wantonly at everything that came by, whatever it was, and however unlikely the mode of transport. I'd seen other hitchhikers before, standing with place names written on bits of paper, and anything was worth a try so I found a piece of soft card in my rucksack about eighteen inches by twelve and drew '3 WAYS' on it in tall letters with a blue biro. On the other side of it was a poster about flying that my parents had sent me and on one corner there was some of my mother's handwriting: 'A gift from Bakewell Show'. For some unknown reason this piece of card survived my travels along with my diaries, and it hangs in my study today.

I stood by the road proudly and optimistically holding my bit of card aloft but all it seemed to do was arouse expressions of bemusement from the drivers as they sped past me. I filled my water bottle at the tap several times as I waited around in the increasingly hot sun. I was wearing cut-off jeans shorts, hiking boots, thick socks and a t-shirt. After midday I realised I was filling my plastic bottle and drinking a full litre of water *every hour* standing there in the open sun. I thought of the movie *The Bridge on the River Kwai* when the Allied prisoners were forced to stand in the sun all day by the Japanese, and some of them started to pass out. I hoped I'd be alright, provided I kept on drinking. My head was hot and I didn't have any sunglasses, I never did, so I had to screw up my eyes into very thin slits in order to see. Again the skin on my face and arms felt like it was being roasted over a coal fire. How long could I stand this? *There must be a lift soon*, I kept thinking to myself.

Eventually it was six o'clock again, and I'd been standing there in the sun for a full eight hours. Just before dark I decided I'd been there long enough and returned to the same campsite, where I immediately pitched my tent and fell into the wonderful pool. The dust and sweat from my shorts and the rest of my body left a trail of dirt and a film of grease across the surface of the water in my wake. The areas of my legs, arms and face exposed to the sun the most now really were very deeply tanned and had the texture and appearance of an old leather army boot. I splashed around in the cool water, thinking about the day just gone. Could Mount Isa be the location for some of the most difficult and challenging hitchhiking in the whole of Australia, or possibly the whole world? The water in the pool was fantastic and invigorating of course, and after a swim I ate well again at the café on the campsite before settling down inside my tent for some sleep.

Another cool night followed, though it wasn't quite as cold as my first at Mount Isa. The wind had dropped and I was better prepared for it. In the morning I felt extremely low at the prospect of spending another day standing in the hot sun. I packed my rucksack with slow resignation rather than excited anticipation. I trudged through the town back towards the tap and my hitching place for contemplation of a third day.

To my horror I could see another hitchhiker standing near the tap, and obviously making full use of it, so I stopped and hung back a discreet distance. Sadly the stranger wasn't someone I knew from Ron's Ute, so I made no effort to approach and make conversation. I stood a hundred yards away, breaking the rules myself by standing closer to the town so that I was first in line. Vehicles passed continuously but didn't stop. I began to feel as though I was trapped in some infinite loop in time and space, standing near the same piece of road for days, weeks, or even for the rest of my life, like a bizarre science fiction story or an episode from *The Twilight Zone*. If it exists at all, could this be what hell is like?

After two hours with no success I turned around and walked back into the town. A decision had to be made, and I had just made it, but whether it was the right thing to do or not I had absolutely no idea. I stepped inside an Ansett Airlines travel office on the main street and without much hesitation I bought a single bus ticket to Darwin for $75. I'd walked past the office and had seen this advertised in the window the day I arrived but never imagined I wouldn't get a lift. But now it seemed The Isa had beaten me and I wasn't afraid to admit it. The bus was due to leave later that same afternoon. I would just be incredibly glad to finally get out of the place.

The Darwin bus set off on time at three fifteen that afternoon. It was a large plush and very luxurious *Greyhound* coach with a toilet at the rear. At least it *seemed* luxurious compared to the interior of my tiny little tent. I caught a very quick glimpse of the tap by the road as the bus roared past. I was very glad to see it disappear behind me, but I couldn't help feeling slightly upset that I was cheating by taking the bus. The hitchhiker had also gone. I wondered if he'd been lucky, had simply given up, or had died in the heat and was slumped by the road somewhere. I would never know.

Sunset across the Barkly Tableland was a magical display of strong colours: well, differing shades of red, mainly. A deep red earth and a blood red sky, all stretched forever across the huge seemingly limitless expanse of land as far as the eye could see, and for hour after hour. The window of the bus became a view to an incredible world I'd never seen before. The Sinai came close, as did parts of the Negev Desert, but central Australia was true wilderness.

What I perceived to be real Aborigines were seen occasionally in groups walking near the road, with no transport and no houses anywhere near they must therefore have been 'real'. There was nothing out there, so where were they going to sleep? What were they doing out there, in the middle of nowhere? It was then as we passed Camooweal and entered the Northern Territory that I must have fallen asleep, my head vibrating very gently on the tinted glass of the window next to me. The huge bus was quiet except for some low road noise and the soft rhythmic hum of the engine, and there were some dim lights in the floor down the centre gangway, which altogether created a warm and cosy atmosphere.

The bus hissed and groaned to a halt in the dark and the driver flung the door open. "Half an hour, okay? Stretch yer legs, and get sumpen t'eat," and he jumped down out of the bus, followed immediately by a few bleary-eyed passengers. We were outside a building which had a flickering neon sign perched in the middle of a sloping corrugated iron roof which read: 'Barry Caves Roadhouse'. It was a twenty-four hour café, populated by truckers and tourists, and anyone else passing by.

I gathered my senses and stepped down from the bus. I wandered inside with some of the other passengers and bought a portion of chips and a cup of sweet tea from a big sweaty man behind the counter wearing a filthy white apron. I then sat near the door to eat my midnight feast gazing out at the blackness. The cheap tables and chairs were dragged noisily around on the peeling linoleum floor, and beyond the fly screens huge moths danced and wheeled around a single bright bulb in a conical-shaped, blue enamel shade hanging above the door. There was nothing else around this one building, and there were no other buildings. There was simply nothing, for hundreds of miles in any direction. I tried to think of another place I'd visited in my life that was as remote as this, but I couldn't.

Back in my seat and with a full stomach I fell asleep again very quickly once the bus had resumed its journey. While I was asleep we turned north at the famous Three Ways junction onto the Stuart Highway. Darwin was just a quick hop north now, only about another 600 miles, or 1,000 kilometres or thereabouts, no distance at all for Australia.

Just before dawn most people including me were awake when the driver pointed out a turn off on the right to an interesting tourist site known as the 'We of the Never Never Graves'. We of the Never Never was an autobiographical novel written by a woman called Jeannie Gunn in 1902, when she was one of the first white women to settle in the area. It was a tough enough place in modern times so she must have been through some desperate hardship, with a very interesting story to tell, hence the book. Hard times can obviously provoke some great literature. There was a brief stop in a town called Katherine to pick up and unload, and then onward the remaining 200 miles or 350 kilometres to Darwin.

From the dry dusty heat of the desert the air-conditioned bus drove into the high humidity of the tropical Top End, as Darwin and the rest of the Northern Territory was known. The heat and very high humidity meant that almost every building of any significance was completely air-conditioned. This was the tropics, and it was very hot all year round. Across the Timor Sea only a few hundred miles away were the islands of Indonesia and Java. Darwin was so close to these far eastern locations that during the Second World War the Imperial Japanese Air Force bombed it dozens of times.

I had finally arrived in Darwin. I was extremely excited at being there and was very keen to get started looking for work. I couldn't possibly have known what fate had in store for me.

THE TOP END

Darwin

I saw an ideal campsite from the window of the bus flash past me on the way into the city, so once we reached our destination I started walking back to find it. I tried thumbing but no-one was interested. Drivers weren't to know that I only wanted a lift for a few miles. Eventually I found The Shady Glen Caravan Park about three miles from the city centre and bought a pitch for seven dollars a night. I paid for a week in advance, which on reflection was quite foolhardy and overoptimistic, as it left me with very little money.

The Darwin heat was almost unbearable, so I was very pleased to see a small open-air pool on the camp site, which I suspected I would use quite a lot. I had a plan of action, of sorts, in that I would try to find employment as soon as possible. I felt quite confident too. Darwin was thousands of miles from anywhere so who else would have thought of travelling there for work? If I was successful then who knows, maybe I'd stay?

Sadly there wasn't a café at the caravan site, but there was a small general store, so I bought a large loaf of sliced white bread. Unable to think of anything else to put on the bread I also bought a huge plastic tub of beef dripping, and a litre of milk. The dripping was probably the most ridiculous and inappropriate item I've ever bought in my life. It was animal fat and so how did I realistically think that it would stay edible for very long in such intense tropical heat?

I pitched my tent and then wearing my shorts I jumped into the pool. There were lots of screaming kids in the water, which was warm and tasted very salty like sweat, or urine. There must have been a lot of sweat in it, but the main reason for the salty taste was most probably the fact that it was a salt-water pool. Either that or I was indeed swimming in six feet of sweat and piss.

After a lovely swim and a look around the wonderful campsite I had bread and dripping for tea washed down with warm homogenised milk. Then even before dark I climbed into my tent and fell asleep. I was relieved to have reached Darwin, thousands of miles from Brisbane, but I was exhausted too. After an undisturbed and very warm night I woke up with the dawn and to the sound of human activity around me in the campsite. I felt reassured by these sounds of other people, but then I remembered what I had to do. I needed a job urgently, and this would be my first full day of job seeking.

I unzipped the inner fly-sheet to reach for my tub of dripping for breakfast. For some reason I just managed to check my hand before it touched anything. The area of grass inside the fly sheet where the tub should have been was a seething mass of insects of varying sizes, all climbing about on the dripping, pulling at one another to get closer in a silent insect free-for-all. The tub was nowhere to be seen and was presumably underneath the writhing mound which consisted in the main of some very large black and dark brown cockroaches. I'd obviously not put the lid back on correctly the night before and I was horrified to see that I'd been sleeping with these things crawling about only a few inches from my head. I couldn't even attempt to rescue the dripping and so I just left it, abandoning it to the avaricious wildlife. Luckily I'd brought the bread inside the tent with me, but in the heat it had become soggy and warm, and didn't smell particularly good.

Another unwanted surprise came when I realised my finances were getting desperately low, and were much worse than I first thought. I needed to be decisive because my money was almost gone. I would soon be in some serious trouble if I wasn't careful and so I had to do something quickly. I'd wasted money on a large tub of beef dripping that had only been partially consumed by me and my insect friends, and which now had to be thrown away. It was also giving off a very strange smell too, so even without the insects it had definitely become unfit to eat.

I'd spent too much on the campsite, and I hadn't really budgeted for spending $75 on a ticket to get to Darwin. How would the campsite have known anyway if I'd overstayed a few days without paying? It was a busy place and they would surely never have noticed. I couldn't go to the office now and say I was leaving and ask for my money back, unless I did that and then moved somewhere else? It was a possibility I could consider, but I didn't see another campsite, and there might not even be one nearby. I couldn't live in my tent without some facilities either, not in that heat and in those conditions, so I came to the conclusion that I had to stay where I was.

At that moment I made a decision as to how I could obtain some quick cash. I stood at the campsite gates and stuck out my thumb. I started walking towards town as I hitched and was picked up quite quickly. In the centre of the city I had a brief look around and I reluctantly sold my Walkman in a booming pawn shop for just $20. It had cost me £80 in England, and granted it had a few scratches on it after two years use, but I felt as though I'd been robbed by selling it for that little. I had no choice.

I returned to the campsite on foot but relieved that I was a little fluid again. I washed my clothes in a large stainless steel sink in the shower block, scrubbing the armpit areas of my t-shirts thoroughly with my soap. This used a huge amount of the soap and I noticed it was wearing away incredibly quickly. My socks smelt particularly unpleasant and when the first pair were dry after washing it was a wonderful sensation to put clean ones on again.

Instead of beef dripping for breakfast I bought a tin of baked beans, something I should have done in the first place, and I opened it using the blade on my penknife. This is not as difficult as it might sound. If you stab the top of the tin and haul the blade around slowly with a sawing motion it will open quite easily. It might blunt the blade a little every time you do it though, and you have to hold the tin and the knife very firmly or you risk tearing your hand apart. Necessity is the mother of invention, as the saying goes, and it was the first time I'd ever done it, but opening a tin in this way was a skill that has stayed with me ever since. I ate a few slices of dry bread with the beans, and I used a plastic tea spoon which I'd found earlier on the campsite to extract the last of the beans from the tin. It tasted pretty good actually.

I'd almost run out of cigarettes too, which in a way seemed worse than not having much food. It seemed you always had a friend and a tiny luxury if you at least had a smoke. I didn't want to spend precious food money on cigarettes, so when they ran out I decided I'd have to go without, again I had no choice. I had to keep a few dollars in reserve for food. Things were beginning to look quite grim.

After breakfast I lazed around in the pool waiting for my clothes to dry and while trying to decide what to do. Then I made a lengthy diary entry before I put on a clean, dry, but very crumpled t-shirt and my skimpy little denim shorts which had just about dried from swimming in the pool. I then hitch-hiked into Darwin, and was lucky to get a good lift almost straight away.

When I reached the centre of Darwin I was still very optimistic about finding work and quite by chance I found the CES, the Commonwealth Employment Service office. When I walked into the CES, the 'casual' section was packed with people, mainly young lads around my age, all seemingly desperate to find work. I looked at them in astonishment. How could this be? Where had they all come from? They must have heard similar wild unsubstantiated rumours about plenty of work with high pay, just as I had. It seemed there weren't any casual jobs available; the few that had existed earlier in the day had all gone.

I was stunned, and suddenly feeling very despondent I walked across the road to the main Post Office, and into the *Post Restante*. Maybe someone had sent me something? Maybe, just on the off chance, Dave had sent me some paintings I could sell? But this was ridiculous, who even knew I was in Darwin? I'd told people this was where I was heading but no-one could have known that I'd actually arrived. It is quite amazing the strange hopes a person can cling onto when desperation ensues. I returned to the CES again, with rapidly decreasing optimism. There were still huge queues everywhere so I decided to return to the campsite. I noted that the CES was open at eight o'clock every morning, so I knew I had to ensure that I was back there the next day very early, just when the doors opened.

I bought another tin of beans and opened it with my penknife. Sadly my bread had turned so I had to buy another loaf. This was to be my lunch and evening meal. The shop on the campsite was expensive, but I hadn't seen any large supermarkets and so I was stuck with paying inflated prices. I thought of all the lovely meals of sausages and eggs I'd been eating on my trip up until then, and wondered why I hadn't kept a closer eye on my diminishing finances. That night any initial feelings of optimism I still had slowly drained away as the stark reality of my situation struck me. I was at the very top end of Australia where I didn't know anyone, and I had virtually no money. What on earth was I doing?

In the morning I rose with the sun. The shop was open so I bought another tin of beans and ripped the top off with my knife. Several cold baked bean sandwiches later I was on the road walking and thumbing into town. No-one picked me up but I didn't particularly mind; I'd woken up with a headache and could feel a cold brewing so I thought the early morning walk might help to clear my head. I arrived at the CES office early, just after it had opened. I was very surprised and deeply disappointed when I saw the casual section was already inundated with hopeful job seekers, and the first of that day's quota of unskilled jobs had already been taken. This was a terrible blow, and I didn't quite know what to do. In desperation and as a matter of idle curiosity I looked at the clerical section. Amazingly, there was a job advertised in a branch of the Commonwealth Bank which appeared to be exactly the same role I had at Lloyd's Bank years before in England. I took the card and noted the address.

The bank was smart and clean, and wonderfully air-conditioned. I must have appeared like *Crocodile Dundee's* poor relation and utterly incongruous when I stomped in: a deep tan, badly crumpled t-shirt, cut off denim shorts, knotted dry hair and huge hiking boots. I introduced myself to the staff at the enquiry desk and nervously showed them my CES employment card. To one or two ill-disguised looks of complete surprise, to which I also add myself in that number, I was ushered inside and told to sit at a large encoding machine in their busy open-plan office. I sat down in full view of both staff and public and felt incredibly self-conscious. In front of me was a similar machine to the one I'd operated before, a lifetime ago, at the bank in Grantham. Great bundles of cheques had to be typed singly into the machine as quickly as possible using a giant key pad. I found it unusually difficult that morning and despite my very best efforts I failed miserably.

While I was sitting in the bank I realised I had developed a severe headache, a raging sore throat and I felt a bad head cold had already started to grip my body. I was in the hottest place I'd ever been to in my life and I had caught a cold from somewhere. I was also hungry and thirsty. Luckily the bank staff took sympathy and gave me a cup of sweet tea and a biscuit, which cheered me up, and counteracted for the sad but inevitable news that I hadn't got the job. As I sipped my tea I glanced around and saw there were smart young men about my age in sharp business suits sitting close to some lovely ladies in delicate skirts and dresses, all well-fed and happy. I caught a quick glimpse of my own reflection in some polished glass, sitting like a scruffy oaf in my boots and cut-off shorts. I looked as though I might have been there to clean the windows or empty the bins. The bank staff had probably driven to work that morning in their brand new air-conditioned Japanese cars, and not walked 3 miles to get there in the baking, stifling heat as I had done. All credit to them for giving me a chance as they did, but I was laughably unsuitable.

I fled back towards the Shady Glen Caravan Park, trudging

with leaden feet, heavy heart and a throbbing head all the way up the main road. It was then that I did something I'd never done before or even contemplated doing before; I picked up my first cigarette butt. I wouldn't have done it, normally, but the first one I found was almost a full cigarette, just lying there on the pavement in front of me. It would have been a real shame to have left it. I imagined I might have picked it up anyway, even if I had plenty of money, it was such a nice looking cigarette. It really was beautiful and just ripe for the picking. I flicked off a few crumbs of ash from the flattened end where someone had clearly lit it and then for whatever reason had stamped it out almost immediately. I found another a hundred yards later, only half a cigarette this time, and picked it up with great enthusiasm and then dropped it carefully and reverently into the left pocket of my shorts.

I collected quite a few second-hand cigarettes on my way back to the campsite, a small handful actually, and I was very pleased with my crop and believed that I'd been very lucky. I didn't feel in any way like a scruffy hobo, demeaned by collecting these used cigarette butts, quite the contrary. I needed a smoke and this was the only way I could get one, so it just felt right, at the time. It was necessary, essential in fact, and I'd obtained all this tobacco for free! I had thought I wouldn't be able to have a smoke but now I could. It's amazing how you can find justification for just about anything when you really need to.

The shop at the campsite sold cigarette papers, so I bought a packet, along with a box of matches and another tin of beans. I also bought some very expensive flu tablets because I really was feeling terrible. This virtually saw the end of my money. Apart from a few bits of change it was now all gone. I took two huge tablets as big as horse pills from the packet and swallowed them down in water. They were so enormous and my throat was so painful it felt like I was trying to force a couple of barbed golf balls down my neck. I managed to eat the tin of beans and then I hid from the rest of the world inside my tent. I sneezed and coughed and blew my nose, then fell asleep among small piles of snotty tissues, which were quickly seized upon by my insect friends who seemed to enjoy feeding on the gallons of mucus I was producing from my fast-running nose.

I slept for more than twelve hours straight and woke up early the next morning feeling a little better. I then noticed to my dismay that the majority of my bread appeared visibly mouldy on almost every slice but I managed to pick at it and eat some pieces that appeared free of decay. I was still very hungry, but I had nothing else to eat. My teeth felt huge and incongruous in my mouth and they all hurt like hell. I wondered if this was connected to my hunger. I decided I would try to be optimistic, so after taking more flu tablets I set out for the centre of Darwin. I felt very weak so I stuck out my right thumb without walking and was lucky with a lift almost immediately.

Yet again the CES office was crowded and there were no jobs available. I looked around blankly and I admit I had no idea what to do with myself. I'd run out of ideas, but more importantly I'd completely run out of money, I didn't have any food left, and I was desperate. What on earth was I going to do? I was facing some extreme hardship and the very real prospect that I might eventually starve. I couldn't ask for help from the authorities in case they checked my immigration status. It didn't occur to me to commit crime, I was just too weak and I'd probably be hopeless at it anyway.

I found somewhere quiet and sat slumped on the ground in the doorway of a shop not yet open, like a true hobo. Despite my cold I rolled myself a cigarette from the butts I'd found in the street and tried to cheer myself up, but I couldn't help feeling extremely tearful. I couldn't get any lower. I was in dire need of a miracle.

It was then that I had an astonishing piece of good fortune, as though a guardian angel suddenly appeared from nowhere, which he did. I finished smoking my cigarette and was walking back towards the CES when I literally bumped into a Canadian called Mark whom I'd known briefly in Brisbane several months before. Mark was much taller than me and he physically grabbed hold of me by the shoulders and dragged me into a smart air-conditioned shopping precinct nearby where he bought us both a large sweet milky coffee. At that moment this enormous latte seemed like a meal in itself, and as soon as it was finished I was whisked back to his house in the outer suburbs, by car.

When we arrived at his place Mark spent the next twenty minutes demonstrating to me some self-defence moves he'd learnt from somewhere, jumping around on the living room floor like Bruce Lee on acid while I looked on, mildly light-headed with hunger, and feigning sincere interest in my host's rather baffling martial arts movements. His obvious enthusiasm for the subject didn't quite reach me under the circumstances and I felt trapped in a similar manner as when standing at a function and you suddenly realise you have become the target of the local pub bore. Why was he showing me all this karate stuff, didn't he know I was starving?

My mind started to drift, and I wondered if Mark had anything to eat in the house. If he didn't shut up soon and stop leaping about I thought I might kill him for food at any moment, regardless of his karate chops. I started daydreaming about food, any food, and was about to ask Mark about it when coincidentally he broke off from his oriental tumbling and suddenly offered me some lunch. He then made us both some wonderful vegemite on toast topped with generous dollops of peanut butter and honey, and there was an avocado tree in the garden, so we each had a large avocado to follow, all washed down with yet more sweet milky coffee. It was absolutely brilliant and was by far the best meal I'd eaten in days.

Mark couldn't possibly have known the dangerous state of penury I found myself in, but he seemed to guess. We returned to the city centre so that we could both check the CES again, and when we parted an hour later Mark handed me a crisp red twenty dollar note, which was supposedly a loan until we next met. We shook hands warmly, and with the usual earnest exchanges of addresses. Strangely I never saw Mark again, even though I was to remain in Darwin for several more days after this meeting. It was as though he vanished as quickly as he had appeared.

I felt completely revived after my brief encounter with Mark. I spent the rest of that day walking around industrial units knocking on doors asking for casual work, anything, to earn a few quid in a desperate attempt to rescue my situation. I walked several miles in the searing heat, but there was nothing available. At the end of the afternoon I returned to the campsite utterly exhausted and completely deflated.

The next day I tried again. I kept taking my flu tablets until they'd all gone, and I think they probably helped sustain me against the conditions. I trudged for miles to an address given to me by the CES with the possibility of a cleaning job only to find the place didn't exist. I then took a written test in the CES office for a part-time book-keeping job despite being rubbish at maths, only to be told when the perspective employers saw me that the job had been taken.

I finally returned to the caravan park at seven o'clock in the evening, just as a coach party of tourists arrived for an open-air film show about Darwin. I tagged along and listened to the history of the city, from when it was first settled to the present day. In addition to the Japanese bombing in World War Two, Darwin was devastated on Christmas Day 1974 by Hurricane Tracy, which virtually destroyed the entire city.

I woke up the next morning feeling a lot better and quite determined to have one last crack at Darwin. I ripped open another tin of beans that I'd bought with some of Mark's $20 and after breakfast set out for the city. Back at the CES office I very naively and optimistically applied for a job at a sheep station hundreds of miles into the Northern Territory outback. I caught a bus to a different office for the interview in a suburb known as Casuarina, and the farmer was there, interviewing dozens of other hopeful lads just like me. When it came to the crunch I wasn't able to lie. I couldn't tell him that I was great on a horse and that yes, I could muster cattle and sheep, all without a problem. It was obvious I hadn't a clue anyway. The farmer would have been very angry if he'd driven me for hours to the sheep station only to find out that I didn't know one end of a horse from the other. I remember seeing the young lad who had obviously been given the job because I saw him climbing into a Toyota Land Cruiser with the farmer. He had a cowboy hat on his head and cowboy boots on his feet so he already looked the part, unlike me. I thought of the wonderful life he would then have, riding around the vast open spaces living a wild and free cowboy lifestyle just like the characters in the seventies TV series *High Chaparral*.

I contemplated trying to find Mark's address, but I just couldn't remember where it was. I was amazed I'd not seen him again. I bought ten cigarettes which I broke apart and mixed with the butts I'd found so they'd last longer. I also bought more bread and some peanut butter before I returned to my tent. Later that night I lay on my back alone in the salty, sweaty pool drifting around, staring up at the wonderful panoramic view of the stars. I'd come to the end of my time in Darwin, and it was clear that I had to leave. I'd exhausted all possibilities. I'd tried my very best but it just wasn't to be. But where should I go? Brisbane was thousands of miles away, and an incredibly difficult return journey. Where else could I go, and with hardly any money? What on earth should I do?

THE ALICE

"I'm going to The Alice. Do you want a lift?"

I had to get out of Darwin, and there was only one way, south. I'd spent a week in the city and it had been a complete unmitigated disaster. You couldn't even swim in the beautiful warm Java Sea because of deadly 'Sea Wasp' jellyfish floating about in the water, and it was just so incredibly hot all the time, even at night. Things would obviously have been different if I'd managed to get a job, but even so it occurred to me then that it takes a special kind of person to live up there at the Top End, and all credit to those who do. In the words of the old Aussie saying about the place, 'Someone has to live there!'

I spent a leisurely morning contemplating my next move and took a last enjoyable swim in the pool. My cold had all but gone, and I felt a lot better. I shaved but left a little goatee beard on my chin and a moustache, which would stay for the rest of my time in Australia. I bought more sliced bread and half a dozen cans of baked beans then I dismantled my little home from home. I opened one of the cans and ate the contents with some bread for breakfast. I didn't want hunger pains to ruin my trip, and my rucksack then felt unusually heavy with the extra weight of the remaining five cans and the peanut butter.

By the time I was ready to stand back out on the road it was almost midday. It was not the best time to start hitchhiking, but a good lift could actually appear at any moment, so I wasn't too worried. It was great to be looking in the opposite direction to Darwin city at last, and it felt good to be on the move again. It was a wonderful feeling to be able to pack everything away and move on so easily, and it's a shame that for most of us our lives usually do not contain this amount of personal freedom. They say that some vagrants truly love their homeless way of life due to the total autonomy that comes with it, and I can just about understand this now. I also surprised myself at how happy I felt, particularly after enduring so much hunger and disappointment. But maybe it was the vanquishing of such hardship that had revived my spirit, making me stronger and more determined.

After only twenty minutes two lads pulled up in a bright red Holden Ute and took me on board. They introduced themselves as Rod and Ritchie. Ritchie had the nickname 'Crunchy', which he seemed very proud of but didn't explain. They were both very lively and happy, and were just the tonic I needed. As the Ute gathered speed leaving Darwin quickly behind they asked me where I was heading, and what I was hoping to do. I told them that I was going to be an author, and that one day I would write them into a book, for their part giving me a lift from Darwin to Katherine. They were both thrilled to hear their names would eventually appear in a best-selling travel book about Australia, and to celebrate in anticipation Rod pulled out an enormous pre-rolled spliff from inside the glove box, which he then proudly lit with great ceremony before passing it around.

The spliff consisted entirely of Sinsemilla leaf, so he said, and it certainly had a very strong taste. I took several long pulls on it and settled down for a comfortable ride all the way to Katherine. Rod put a *Rolling Stones* tape into the car stereo just as the THC began to fill my blood wonderfully after a long absence. Sitting next to these two guys in the cab of the Ute I glanced around and noticed the vinyl on the dashboard in front of me was badly faded and split in places, no doubt due to the persistent heat and strong sunshine, but otherwise their Ute was a fantastic machine. The engine sounded loud and throaty, as though it had been highly tuned, and it seemed to growl beautifully like a Sumatran tiger every time Ritchie hit the gas pedal.

As we drove further south we had the windows wound fully down so the great clouds of thick cannabis smoke whirled around our heads momentarily before being sucked away in the draught. The breeze from the open windows was incredibly warm as it blasted into the Ute, so much so that it actually felt just like very hot air from a hair dryer, and I'd never experienced anything like it before. The spliff very quickly began to have a wondrous effect on me. To add to the marvellous sequence of events Ritchie then threw an arm under his seat and as if by magic produced three tins of beer from nowhere. By another strange miracle all the tins were ice cold. Just as Mick Jagger began singing 'Start me up' I opened a tinny and took my first swig of beer. Darwin was already miles behind and forgotten, and my day could hardly get any better.

It's quite a way from Darwin to Katherine, about 250 miles or around 400 kilometres, and so we didn't reach the town until six o'clock that night. It had been another one of those perfect lifts that I was sad to see come to an end. I was dropped on the south side of town, at my request, and after some hearty hand-shaking and mutual good wishes Rod and Ritchie turned around and drove back into town. The Australian outback roads are so linear and uneventful that Rod and Ritchie's idea of getting bombed on beer and dope certainly helped to pass the time. Not that I would recommend it while driving of course.

I stood by the road in the Northern Territory twilight wondering what to do. It was very warm and I still felt quite detached from reality after the smoke and beer, which had continued on and off for most of the journey, so I decided to continue hitchhiking. The next major town was Alice Springs in the very centre of Australia, and was at least 700 miles or 1,200 kilometres away. Looking at my map I decided that the town just south of Three Ways, Tennant Creek, had to be my next realistic objective.

As I stood alone by the road a small group of Aborigine men and women slowly ambled past me, as though they had all the time in the world. Two of the older ones stopped and asked me for a cigarette, which I was happy to give them. I rolled the three of us one each even though my own supply was virtually back to nil again. They stayed with me to smoke, and they asked me where I was going and where I was from. Seeing them up close I could see their faces were lined with some very deep creases like the ruts in a freshly ploughed English field, and their skin was black, not dark brown, but jet black. I then noticed others sitting in groups under gum trees near the road and the two I was with very kindly offered me some food if I didn't get a lift quickly.

Just then a very smart and shiny four-by-four police truck emerged from the town and as soon as they saw it approach the Aborigines left me and walked away towards the trees. The truck pulled up quite close to me and two white male Northern Territory cops climbed out and walked over to me.

"G'day. Got any ID on yer mate?" one of them said, looking at me intently. I looked back at them in turn and then across at the Aborigines, and then the other cop said:

"You don't wanna talk to that lot, mate, stay well clear if I were you, eh?" I handed them my Queensland driving licence and they both scanned it in turn before handing it back. "You're hitchhiking are ye?" one of them said.

"Aww yeah... down to the Alice I reckon," I replied, in my best and most convincing Queensland accent.

"Okay, but be careful, eh? Stay away from the Abbos. They'd rob ye as soon as look at ye."

They were polite and business-like, if a little racist, and repeated their advice to be careful before they climbed back aboard their truck. They then turned it around smartly, and drove off back towards town. The group of Aborigines wandered off further into the near distance and sat down again. I continued hitching without success until nine o'clock that night before I gave up for the day. I walked about three hundred yards into the town and pitched my little tent on a quiet piece of parched green that looked like a public park area.

After eating a tin of beans I slept well all night and woke up just before dawn. There was a calm sunrise when I packed the tent away into my rucksack, and it then went on to become a splendid Northern Territory morning. I could see more groups of Aborigines had reappeared and were sitting together in the shade of some gum trees dotted all around quite close to the road. They seemed to wander about taking no notice of roads and fences, as their ancestors had done for thousands of years. They reminded me of the Bedouin Arabs I'd seen in the deserts of the Middle East, living a life apparently separate and unhurried.

I rationed myself to just a couple of slices of bread and peanut butter for breakfast before setting out on the road again. I could immediately tell that it was going to be a very hot day as the morning progressed. Sweat ran down the inside of my clothing, which stuck to me in damp areas wherever it touched. Salty drops fell into my eyes causing them to sting so much I couldn't see properly.

My water bottle was already almost empty, and it was only ten o'clock in the morning. A man in a jeep stopped briefly only to inform me that if I was still there at ten o'clock that night he'd pick me up. Hopefully I wouldn't be, but it was quite reassuring to know that in twelve hours or so if I was still stranded that at least I would get somewhere.

I had to plan the day. Clearly I was going to be there for quite a while. I could have another awful three day Mount Isa experience ahead of me, but this time I didn't have any money for a bus or any other means of escape. If the man *didn't* come back later and I was still there, what would I do? I broke the day up into manageable segments, and decided I would eat at three o'clock and then again at nine, if I was still there. It also gave me something to keep on looking forward to. I had the wondrous sum of fifteen dollars left, half a loaf, some peanut butter, several tins of beans, and enough tobacco for a couple of thin cigarettes. I was okay for the moment. I could last one more day, maybe two at the most.

Not long after my first scheduled three o'clock feed a large old car pulled up and the driver leaned across and looked at me through the open passenger window:

"Where are you going?" he shouted at me.

"South… anywhere south!" I shouted back

"I'm going to The Alice. Do you want a lift?"

"Yeah, sure, that'd be great, thanks!" and so I picked up my rucksack and opened the car door. The driver introduced himself as Raymond, and after an instantaneous hitchhiker's kerbside judgment in which I decided he seemed to be a nice bloke and wasn't intent on killing me, I jumped in. It was 350 miles or 600 kilometres to Tennant Creek, down a long straight road with no civilization in between.

I settled down in my seat for the long journey and conversation in the car centred on the dramatic emptiness of the surroundings as we passed the 'We of the Never Never Graves' again, down into the central Northern Territory, and to the edge of the Barkly Tableland. It looked as spectacular in its vast emptiness then as it had done the first time I'd seen it a week before, when I was still hopeful of something positive happening in Darwin. Ray told me that he wasn't surprised I hadn't found work in Darwin, it was the only major city for thousands of miles and it was quite wrong to just turn up expecting to find something, as so many obviously did. Who'd want to anyway? It's so damned hot!

As we drove along it seemed Ray's car window wouldn't wind up to the top, which was not a problem most of the time, except for the last few hours after dark when it started to get slightly cooler. I wrapped my shoulders in my sleeping bag to keep out the chill.

We passed the Three Ways junction and soon after that we arrived at Tennant Creek, just before nine o'clock at night. Ray booked into a motel with a twin room, two single beds, at $47 for the night.

"I don't expect any money, don't worry. I'd be staying here anyway..." Ray told me, so I laid claim to one of the beds in the room. Realistically I had no money to offer, and Ray knew this. In gratitude I gave Ray my parent's address in England, telling him to call in if passing, which was highly unlikely, and we both knew it. But the offer was there, and that was the important thing. Luckily, to this day no-one has ever turned up unannounced at my parents' house demanding a bed for the night in exchange for what had been given to me.

Ray disappeared for a few minutes and returned to the room with a huge bag of greasy but delicious chips covered in salt and vinegar which he insisted we shared. I had no idea where he got these from but I wasn't really bothered. In return I provided some of my bread and we ate several wonderful chip butties for dinner. I then used the facilities in the room and it was the first proper shower I'd taken for days with some decent soap and shampoo, and the first bed with clean sheets I'd slept in for weeks.

It was nice to smell vaguely sweet again. My deodorant had long since run out, and it was not a priority so I guess I didn't smell too good most of the time. It is one of the strangest things about such travelling that you might think your own body odour would grow geometrically worse as you continue to sweat day after day in the same clothing, but I don't think this actually happens. Instead it reaches a certain level where it stabilises, and then the pong you give off becomes a combination of several pungent smells such as bad breath, general body odour, unclean clothes, tobacco smoke and many accretions of stale sweat, amongst other things. Eventually you have a generic kind of unpleasant whiff about you rather than simply stinking of armpit body odour.

I slept very well that night, and then in the morning I shared more of my bread and peanut butter with Ray in the room before we set off. There were tea and coffee facilities in the room too so we had a pretty decent breakfast. I guess he could have eaten a breakfast provided by the motel at some extra cost but he clearly didn't want to do this.

It was still another 300 miles or 500 kilometres to Alice Springs. Ray fuelled up the car and checked the radiator and tyres. He paid particular attention to the tyres. We couldn't afford a blow-out in the middle of nowhere. It wouldn't just be inconvenient; it could actually become potentially life-threatening. He had a spare that was pumped up and ready to use, just in case, and the jack was in full working order. We set off at a very civilised and leisurely nine-thirty, heading south on the Stuart Highway.

After a couple of hours we passed a remarkable rock formation near the road that Ray told me was called 'The Devil's Marbles'. These consisted of some enormous rounded boulders clumped together in a group, as the name suggested, like huge rock marbles. Typically with nothing else around they looked particularly incongruous as though randomly dumped there by some angry giant. They were an interesting and an eerie sight.

It became quite an event to see another vehicle, particularly one passing in the opposite direction. I felt as though all fellow travellers we saw were kindred spirits of some kind, each battling the extreme elements, pioneering in our own small way across the great empty wilderness. When another vehicle did pass in the opposite direction even on the smooth tarmac surface clouds of red dust followed which blew into the car through Ray's open and uncloseable window. Everything in the car eventually became coated in a fine layer of this red dust and I could taste it on my lips and in the back of my throat.

Hours passed which saw us driving through a vast emptiness on what must have been one of the loneliest roads in the world. We rarely saw anyone travelling in our direction, and it was there that I saw more of the huge road trains than anywhere else, thundering along looking monstrous and unstoppable.

Our safe arrival in Alice Springs felt like a real achievement. We drove into the town in mid-afternoon and my first impression was how quiet it seemed. It was very hot of course, so no doubt those who could were inside enjoying their air-conditioning. Ray gave me a quick tour of the town, mainly because it was his home, and he seemed to be very proud of it. I was shown the headquarters of The Royal Flying Doctor Service and I realised by looking at my map that we really were virtually in the dead centre of the whole continent. In fact Ray told me proudly that *The Alice* as Alice Springs was known, was very nearly equidistant from Darwin in the north and Adelaide in the south, being almost 1,000 miles or 1600 kilometres from each.

Greenery was sparse and reserved for small and well-manicured lawns and the hardiest of gum trees, and the earth *really was* a deep red ochre colour, hence the nick-name for the region, *The Red Centre*. I was wondering why it had been decided to build a town in such a remote and inhospitable place, and I was about to ask Ray when he stopped the car on a bridge overlooking the Todd River. Looking out across from the bridge I could see there was no water in the river at all, not even a drop or a tiny trickle. Ray explained that at times of rare heavy rain it would look more like a river, but the entire town's water supply came mainly from the natural springs, and it was named after these and a woman called Alice, the wife of an early pioneer Sir Charles Todd. I was incredibly grateful to Ray for the lift and his brief but informative tour of the town. I felt as though I knew the place quite well already. Ray spun the car around and dropped me at my request on Alice's south side. You can only say thank you to someone and really mean it once, but in this instance I wished I could have said it many more times to Ray.

WOOMERA PROHIBITED AREA

'Travellers on this road are not permitted to deviate'

My next destination was Adelaide. I decided to try for Adelaide rather than return to Brisbane the way I'd already come. I'd not been to South Australia before and I knew an old friend who was somewhere in Adelaide. At least I hoped she was still in Adelaide. I'd not had any contact with her for several weeks, not since before I left Brisbane and so I wasn't completely sure she was still there. I looked inside my rucksack to check that I still had my address book, which I did, and I assumed her address was in there. It was Chrissie, an old girlfriend from my time at Kibbutz Dafna, and it was close to two years since we'd last met. Was I being too headstrong and foolish crossing a continent in order to see an old flame? What if the fire had already gone out?

I sat by the road and made a sign from a sheet of paper I found: 'ADELAIDE'. I tried hitching for several hours with no luck. Adelaide was hundreds of miles away across South Australia, through the Simpson Desert and the Woomera Prohibited Area, where rockets were tested. I'd have to be very lucky again to get a lift across such a huge distance. But I had no choice. I couldn't cheat again by taking a bus, so I just had to wait around for another Raymond, or more lads like Rod and Ritchie in their fabulously equipped Ute.

I continued to have no luck so just before dark I pitched my tent near some public toilets and later that night to my surprise I woke up shivering with cold. Again I couldn't get over the dichotomy of just how hot it was in the daytime but then so cool at night. I was forced to put my jeans on once more and anything else I had with me to keep warm. There was a cool breeze grabbing and pulling at my little tent so I climbed back into my sleeping bag and zipped it up completely.

I woke up after a restless sleep just before dawn and packed away. I was very hungry. I had a few slices of bread left, which was probably on the turn, but which I ate with a tin of beans, and then felt quite a lot better. I found a decent hitching spot on the road out of Alice and began thumbing. As usual there were quite a few large vehicles leaving the town and heading south driving straight past me, and I kept reminding myself that it was a very long drive across a vast wilderness, so I really was in need of a huge amount of luck.

After another hour a shiny black Ute pulled up at my side. The male driver shouted: "Jump in, mate" and so I grabbed the door handle and opened the passenger door. Any lift would be a good lift in these circumstances and so I was very grateful that he had stopped. "I'm going home, to my folk's. They live in Stirling, near Port Augusta..." he said to me. Port Augusta? I probably looked a little puzzled because I'd never heard of either of those towns, so he then said to me: "It's just north of Adelaide. Okay?"

"Yes, thanks, that's great, thanks very much!" I couldn't believe my luck! Almost all the way to Adelaide! Because we knew that we would be together for at least a couple of days as we set off we introduced ourselves. My driver said his nickname was Joe, but that his real name was Adrian. He was in his mid-twenties and had been working as a croupier at a casino in Alice for the last year. He then told me that he'd just split up from his girlfriend of four years, and he'd only just decided a few minutes before to drive home and stay with his parents for a while, almost in a fit of temper. It was obvious he was still angry so I didn't pursue any more personal questions. People's motives for picking up hitchhikers can be many and varied, but having someone repeatedly ask personal questions of them on the journey was probably not one of them. It seemed one long record-breaking lift was to be beaten by the next one; Alice Springs to Adelaide was even further than Katherine to Alice Springs. My guardian angel had struck again.

157

After a couple of hours of uneventful and easy driving, we passed through a tiny hamlet called Erldunda. It's not a well-known place, in fact just like me you've probably never heard of it. It's not popular in itself but for the turn off there from the Stuart Highway. About 180 miles or 300 kilometres to the west is a certain ancient sandstone monolith known as Ayer's Rock. It is also known as *Uluru* which is actually the correct Aborigine name for it. I saw the road sign flash past; *'Ayer's Rock'* and it would be the closest I would ever get to it. If you are hitchhiking you have little say in where the vehicle goes, and Adrian was just not interested in sight-seeing. Even though I really would have liked to have seen it, it just wasn't worth me parting company with Adrian and risking getting stuck out there in the middle of nowhere. It was yet another famous place that I could add to my collection of *almost seen* places!

After another hour we crossed into South Australia from the Northern Territory. There was a clearly defined change between the two states; into South Australia the road surface lost its tarmac covering and the Stuart Highway became a dirt track. It was a very wide and a very smooth dirt track, but dirt none the less, and a fine deep red ochre colour, unmistakably Australia. If it had been quite dusty before, then this was a hundred times worse. Vehicles still managed a good speed though, in fact there didn't seem to be any significant change from the tarmac covered surface, but each car or truck was visible from many miles distant, with huge great billowing clouds of pink-red dust rising up for hundreds of yards behind, disturbed by contact with the wheels. We also passed a waist-high fence which seemed to stretch far away into the distance in a dead straight line. I imagined this fence to be the actual boundary of the two states, cutting across the thousands of empty miles, but I dismissed the idea. It's actually true. It does mark the border between the states and is supposedly rabbit proof, dog proof and emu proof.

Our first stop was at an unlikely sounding place by the name of Oodnadatta. It sounds like something dreamt up for a modern-day episode of *Doctor Who*. It looked quite strange too, located as it was literally in the middle of nowhere. We'd made great time but we needed fuel and to check the state of the engine and tyres. The dirt and dust caused havoc in some vehicles, clogging up the air filters and choking the engines. Coincidentally, and as if to emphasise this, Adrian's Ute coughed and spluttered like a consumptive old man and needed a push start in Oodnadatta. Two hitchhikers, Steve (originally from Hull, England) and a girl called Petroushka (or some such similar name) helped get the Ute going so Adrian then told them they could jump in the back.

It was dark by the time we arrived at the next town, and where it was decided we would stay the night. This really did appear like something from *Star Wars* or some other science fiction movie, and was the very remote and unusual town of Coober Pedy. On arrival there didn't appear to be anything there, with nothing more than a few dozen mounds of light grey earth visible and lights sticking up from the ground. This was because the majority of the buildings were indeed underground, cut into the rock like well-manicured caves in order to avoid the intolerable heat on the surface.

Adrian booked into a motel room – which sadly was not underground – and he went out for food while I stayed in and ate a tin of beans for my dinner. I watched TV in the room and wrote in my diary until Adrian returned. We were both tired so it wasn't long before we turned in for the night. Adrian slept in the double bed while I slept on the floor at the far end of the room. It was wonderful to be indoors again in relative comfort and to use the toilet and shower facilities. My own soap had just about worn away so I needed to use the motel soap to wash. The red dust from the road had laid claim in a thick layer to every inch of my skin and every crevice and crease in my body, and it was a wonderful sensation to be rid of it for a while. The floor of the hotel room was surprisingly comfortable too, and Adrian threw me a soft pillow from the bed so I didn't have to rest my head on my rucksack as I usually did. I felt very lucky indeed.

The other two hitchhikers had wandered off into Coober

Pedy stating they were going to have a look around, which seemed a bit odd in the dark. At the time of my visit the locals told us that it hadn't rained in Cooper Pedy for almost five years. The town's water supply was usually obtained from deep bore holes wherever they could be found, some of which were miles away, and it was also brought in by tanker, making it a very expensive and highly cherished commodity.

In the morning Adrian left the room to go for breakfast and I ate my usual tin of cold beans. After checking out of the motel we met a friend of Adrian's called Len, who was driving a Toyota pick-up and pulling a caravan which apparently had some damaged wheel bearings. Adrian and I helped to lift the caravan, along with the other two hitchhikers who had mysteriously reappeared and seemed to be getting on very well with Len and his mates. We all stood around chatting and commenting on the strangeness of the town and the scenery, while efforts were made to repair the caravan. There was a man-made cave cut deep into the side of a hill which was apparently a church and there were references to opal mining everywhere, for which the town was initially created. During the morning we were joined by others, yet more hitchhikers, who also seemed to appear from nowhere, probably out of the ground. Amanda was a shapely, blonde girl with sharp blue eyes who Adrian took an immediate fancy to. It seemed the attraction was mutual at first as Adrian then decided Amanda should ride with us, more specifically next to him. When it became clear Len's caravan would be repaired imminently we set off with Amanda sitting between Adrian and me. The other hitchhikers remained with Len, with the promise of a lift in his Toyota pick-up truck. Hours had been wasted and it wasn't until the suffocating heat of midday was upon us that we resumed our dusty trek.

A few miles south of Coober Pedy we entered the vast Woomera Prohibited Area. My first thought was how could it be 'prohibited' with a major road running through it? But a large steel sign by the road stated: 'Commonwealth of Australia – PROHIBITED AREA – This road is part of a prohibited area under Defence Forces Regulations – Travellers on this road are not permitted to deviate'. It all sounded rather sinister and suspicious, like the notorious Area 51 in the United States, almost inviting the curious to take a closer look. 'Not permitted to deviate' seemed a strange warning, and I presumed it wasn't just meant to mean 'No sheep shagging'. It formed a huge chunk of central South Australia, as large in area as many small countries, and was reserved for weapons testing and research. At the western side of it around an unfortunate and very remote place called Maralinga the British military conducted atmospheric atomic weapons tests right up until the early 1960s. Not surprisingly the area gained a reputation that was rather euphemistically described as 'a significant radiation hazard' and cost millions to clean up. A fortune was also eventually paid in compensation to the Aboriginal people who owned the land. It is still in use today as a testing area but for conventional weapons only, similar to the British Army's use of Salisbury Plain in England.

There wasn't any air conditioning in Adrian's Ute so every time we passed another vehicle we had to hurriedly close the windows to avoid being covered and choked in thick heavy road dust. Even so I could feel the dry dust again in my hair and in my scalp, up my nose and on my clothing, everywhere in fact. It was a very dry kind of heat again, a desert heat, entirely different to the heat experienced at the Top End in Darwin. I preferred this type of heat; it was at least more bearable than the damp tropical humidity.

Hours later, at Pimba, after 250 miles or 400 kilometres crossing a sea of red dust, we stopped for a leg stretch and to check the vehicle. We were now on the south eastern edge of the Woomera Prohibited Area, having just passed successfully right through it on the highway. It had been disappointingly uneventful. No rockets were seen, or bombs exploding, and sadly it all seemed completely normal.

It was here that Adrian asked me if I wanted to drive. I agreed without hesitation, and was informed that I could drive all the way to Port Augusta. Adrian clearly wanted to devote more of his time in talking to Amanda. We passed some very impressive and extremely wide dry salt lakes on both sides of the road and for hours the terrain was utterly flat and featureless. I'd never been to Utah in the United States at that time and imagined these salt flats to be similar to the ones there. In fact, according to my wonderful map, the intrepid old British speed freak Donald Campbell once drove his machine, Bluebird, across one of them, Lake Eyre in 1964.

It was at Pimba where the road quite suddenly returned to a decent tarmac covering and so the clouds of dust from then on were thankfully reduced. I thoroughly enjoyed the driving, and I hadn't driven anything since Queensland and Ron's Ute with the delayed action steering. Adrian's Ute was luckily in a much better condition!

As I drove on southwards Adrian continued to concentrate all his romantic attentions on Amanda. I gained the impression that though these attentions were perhaps initially reciprocated, they eventually might not bear any significant fruit, even if they did seem to be getting on really well. It was early evening by the time we reached Port Augusta. I remembered Adrian telling me hundreds of miles back that this was to be the end of the line, and I thought he was about to announce our imminent separation when suddenly Adrian suggested we pull into the car park of a motel. I was confused at first but then realised what was happening. I took my rucksack and went in search of a campsite, leaving Adrian and Amanda at the motel.

Port Augusta was clean, tidy and very busy. It was also quite cool compared to the other places I'd recently visited. I found a campsite and walked in through the open gates in the dark, past the office unnoticed, and pitched in a quiet area well away from everyone else. I managed to open a tin of beans and was alarmed to find out while fumbling about in the darkness that it was probably my last one.

After quite a cold night I quickly searched around inside my rucksack in the early morning light and realised my suspicions had been correct in that I had indeed run out of food. I felt a slight wave of panic when I made this discovery. I should have known; my bag was light again and was no longer reassuringly heavy with tins of beans. I remembered how hungry I'd been in Darwin and this was still very fresh in my mind. I found my peanut butter in the bottom of my rucksack but the jar was virtually empty. I scraped out the final remnants until it was all gone, and then I de-pitched, keeping my jeans on rather than my shorts. I left the campsite quickly just before sunrise and before anyone could possibly have known I'd been there. I found this easy to do, both conscience wise, and logistically. When you sleep under canvas or thin nylon in this case, you adapt to night and day very quickly, so it's easy to get up with the sun. I didn't use any of the facilities either, so why should I pay?

I then sat outside the motel for a couple of hours until eight o'clock when Adrian emerged looking very disappointed. He ushered me inside quickly and I gratefully used the toilet and shower before I made us both a large coffee with the facilities provided in the room, putting several heaped spoons of sugar in mine. There were some small packets of biscuits in the tray next to the kettle and these became my breakfast. Adrian then hinted that he had been unsuccessful with Amanda, which was exactly as I had suspected.

Amanda was dropped off outside a Post Office with little ceremony. I then parted company with Adrian not long afterwards, about six miles south of Port Augusta. Addresses were exchanged with the usual earnest intent, but as with so many others we knew we would never meet again. I started hitching with little initial success. An hour passed and it seemed much longer due to the relative cold and the large volume of passing traffic compared to further north. It actually felt like a different country altogether. There were plenty of dark grey clouds being drawn overhead by quite a strong, cool wind, and I began to fear rain might dampen my spirits as well as my clothing. It was all very different to the previous few weeks.

A Ute pulled up and I was made to sit in the back, in the open. I accepted the lift but it was very cold, and I wasn't prepared for it. As the Ute sped along I shuffled up against the back of the cab, shielding myself from the worst of the draught. I was taken 50 miles to Port Pirie, where I then stood for another two hours in the cold wind before a lovely warm car took me almost all the way to the centre of Adelaide, an ideal lift of more than 100 miles, or 160 kilometres.

I bought a street map of the city from a petrol station. Somewhere in my rucksack I had the address of an old girlfriend, a lifeline in whom I could find shelter and some much needed solace, so I opened my address book and began flipping through it. I couldn't find it. I knew she was in Adelaide somewhere but where was her address? It would be an utter disaster if I didn't have it, after just crossing a continent in order to get there. To my horror I could see her address was not in my book where I thought it was. I searched desperately through some tatty papers in the back of my diary and luckily I found her last letter in a small plain brown envelope addressed to the East Brisbane flat. It's a good job that I never throw such personal letters away.

The letter was more than two months old, and I'd not had any contact since. I opened it up and quickly read through it. Chrissie had been quite thorough and it was with a huge sense of relief that I saw the last few lines included her Adelaide address. There were also the words: 'drop me a line...' with a phone number. '*Drop me a line*' didn't exactly sound particularly encouraging. But then why should it? We'd not seen each another for almost two years. We'd not formally broken up though either; I had just left the country to start my great travelling odyssey. Maybe she wasn't even at the address any more? If she wasn't, or if she told me she didn't want to see me, then I really didn't know what I'd do, or what would happen to me. Deep shit again, probably.

ADELAIDE

"What am I doing here on the floor...?"

There were trams in Adelaide which gave the city quite a European, cosmopolitan feel. The hustle and bustle was something of a culture shock from the wide empty deserts of central Australia. I caught two very expensive buses to Modbury North and found the end of Limosa Court. It was late-afternoon and the sun was beginning to ease gently toward the horizon behind the tops of some very tall gum trees. There was a call box at the end of the street. I was very hungry, thirsty, and extremely tired. I was unshaven and my clothes hadn't been washed for days, and not properly for weeks. I felt quite disgusting and probably smelt the same, and I must have appeared more than a little sad and emaciated, like Omar Sharif returning to Varykino in *Dr Zhivago*. Because I'd not worn my jeans much for several weeks I could now feel that they were hanging quite loosely around my waist, and together with my thin pipe-cleaner arms I probably looked like an unconvincing and poorly constructed scarecrow. I'd clearly lost quite a lot of weight.

I stood in the bright and shiny phone box and fumbled in my pockets for some money. To my horror I discovered I had less than a dollar left, only some loose change in fact, which might just be enough to make a single phone call. I counted three twenty cent pieces and some coppers. I put in the first twenty cents and it was credited immediately so I held Chrissie's letter in my left hand and dialled, balancing the receiver in the prominent bones of my right shoulder. The phone started to ring. It rang for an agonisingly long time before it was picked up and a warm, familiar female voice spoke down the line.

"Hello"

"Hello, Chrissie?"

"Yes. Who's this?"

"Have a guess…" There was a pause.

"Jonathan?" The word was drawn out in her wonderful American accent and with a slightly questioning tone at the end.

"Yes. How are you?" I replied, my fake Aussie accent suddenly and noticeably absent, as though abandoned like an empty beer can along the Stuart Highway. Talking to Chrissie immediately made me feel very British again, as it always did.

"I'm fine! How are you? Long-time no speak!" My heart was racing, both at hearing Chrissie's voice and at the thought of actually seeing her again. I was instantly relieved that she was there, but very surprised at just how pleased I was to hear her voice. I must have missed her a lot more than I'd anticipated. Or could it have been the sheer relief in finding out that she was at the address to rescue me from disaster, or a combination of both?

I had to find out if she'd missed me, or even if she would contemplate seeing me again. I was prepared to turn around and walk away if necessary and try to head for Sydney where other friends might be able to help. It would certainly be a long few days without any money or food, but I suppose I could do it if I had to. Chrissie obviously had no idea I was standing just a few yards away at the end of her street.

"You seem pleased to hear from me?" I asked, carefully, probing very gently.

"Of course, why wouldn't I be? Are you still in Brisbane? Where are you?"

"What would you say if I told you I was at the end of your street?"

"Really? *You're here?* You're joking?" There was a pause at which point everything hung momentarily in the balance. "Put the phone down then and get yourself over here!"

I put the receiver back with trembling hands and began walking excitedly up the road. A hundred yards away on the left I saw a figure appear from a front door. Chrissie walked towards me, smiling, and we embraced in the middle of the wide, suburban Adelaide street almost two years since we'd last met. She was the same, though inevitably she appeared a little older, with her long fair hair tied back tightly, smooth to her head. She looked more like a woman than the girl from memory, but her wonderful blue eyes were still the lustrous pools of summer sky that I'd always remembered.

Inside the house I took some crumpled photographs from my diary and handed them one at a time to Chrissie. We sat on the sofa, together but not too close, and she laughed with me, and occasionally at me and not always in a complimentary manner, or so I thought.

I may just have been slightly paranoid due to my current impoverished condition, and I wished circumstances were different. There's no doubt that I must have looked awful and was perhaps not the freshest smelling person she'd ever met. She stood up and walked over to the kitchen to make tea. She was wearing a tight pencil skirt and her legs were slim and sublime. I wanted to take hold of her and hug her and kiss her as though it was the end of the world and there was no time left. But all my soft edges had been rounded off after more than two years of travelling, and my true feelings were well protected beneath a hardened but patchy veneer of emotional calm. Scratch the surface and just underneath it all I was burning with desire for her, and I wanted to hold onto her forever, to stay with her and never leave. I dare not reveal any of this though; I just didn't feel as though I could.

The house belonged to Gerry's brother, Ronald, who was a geologist connected to the oil industry. I'd met Gerry years before in Seattle when I flew over there to visit Chrissie, the year after the kibbutz. After several cups of sweet tea I took a shower and Chrissie put all my clothes on to wash; one pair of jeans, my jeans shorts, two pairs of underpants, three pairs of socks and two t-shirts. I borrowed some of Gerry's trousers and a shirt that was far too big. But it wasn't a large sized shirt, it just hung on my skeletal frame in the same way it would on the back of a tall dining chair. It wasn't until then that I really noticed just how thin I had become. In the mirror it was easy to count my ribs. Throughout the previous two years I must have steadily lost weight, a process that may have been greatly accelerated in the last few weeks. Standing in one spot sweating profusely in the hot sun for hours on a single daily tin of baked beans clearly shed the pounds and was a quick way to lose weight, but I wouldn't recommend it.

Gerry and Ronald arrived home after an hour. I still didn't know anything about Chrissie's current personal circumstances. I daren't ask. Was she seeing Ronald? What was the connection? Was she seeing anyone at the moment? I didn't feel inclined to ask any personal questions and was simply enjoying the luxury of being in a comfortable house after weeks of living rough. The first thing I noticed was how good it was to walk in bare feet on soft thick carpet, to feel the luxurious pile between my toes, and then to sit in a huge, leather armchair.

I glanced across the room and through the open door into the hallway where I could just see the tops of my tent poles protruding from inside my rucksack near the front door. For a brief anxious moment scattered images of all my recent adventures flashed through my mind, many of them good but quite a few of them bad. My body quivered just a little to think that I would be returning to that life very soon, but for now I was in some lovely, homely surroundings and Chrissie had prepared a meal of chicken and pasta, with chilled white wine. It was the best meal I'd eaten for weeks, and was even better than Mark's vegemite on toast in Darwin.

My shrunken stomach felt uncomfortable with so much food inside it, and I was surprised at how little I could manage. My hosts seemed genuinely interested in my recent exploits at the Top End and I suspected they might have actually admired me for it, even if it had largely been a failure. More wine was opened after the meal and the discussions ranged from U.S. – Australian relations to the Australian welfare system and appropriately, immigration. I was extremely tired and could barely stay awake. I hadn't drunk any alcohol since the beer during Rod and Ritchie's lift to Katherine, so my head was swimming. No-one seemed to notice how tired I was. Maybe they just assumed I was this quiet all the time?

It wasn't until midnight that Ron and Gerry decided they were going to bed. I was told I could spread out my thin nylon sleeping bag on the bedroom floor at the back of the house. There were no spare beds but I insisted I didn't mind. I had no idea whose room it was until Chrissie walked in, shut the door behind her, and began to undress. I lay in my sleeping bag trying my very best to appear not to be watching, but it was very difficult. The sight and sound of Chrissie undressing at that moment was the greatest and most wonderful thing on earth. I noticed Chrissie was just wearing a baggy night shirt when she reached up and switched off the light with a quick flick of her wrist and climbed into bed.

It wasn't particularly dark with plenty of suburban light pollution filling the room from the window. We talked for several minutes. It seemed she didn't have a boyfriend at the time, and so was completely free and unattached, as I was. The conversation stayed well away from any further personal issues, but it was clear neither of us were falling asleep very quickly, despite the fact that I was so very tired. Her voice sounded as sweet and mellifluous as it usually did and though I was only a few feet away I wanted to get even closer. But the passage of time and absence of regular contact had built an almost tangible wall between us. We were unfamiliar with each other again, friends and yet strangers at the same time. We were once so close and yet now the usual unspoken casual familiarity was missing and permission for intimate physical contact with Chrissie was absent, faded away, lost somewhere in the passage of time since we were last together. The tiny distance between us felt more like a million miles and I wondered what it would take to overcome this awful situation. One of us had to say and do something, to break this agonising stalemate. Eventually I turned my head towards her and spoke across the room.

"What am I doing here on the floor?" I said, tentatively,

daring to think that I might get a positive reaction. I had to ask, I had to try and take a chance, what had I got to lose? The brief silence that followed seemed to last for hours and my words drifted around in the air between us delicately but shockingly like a string of swear words in a packed church. Had I said something wrong?

"Do you want to come up here then?" Chrissie suddenly replied, quickly followed with some obvious enthusiasm by: "Come on, get in here with me..." just as I could see she'd thrown the covers back from the bed. I stood up and abandoned the sleeping bag on the floor, as comfortable as it was on the thick shag pile carpet. I *was* prepared to sleep down there, just as much as I'd been prepared to turn around at the end of the street earlier that day and head for Sydney, if that was what she'd wanted. But she didn't.

I thought it very surprising and quite wonderful that two years had passed between us and the intervening time was suddenly reduced to nothing at all, as though our last encounter was only the day before, or even just that same afternoon. So much had happened in both our lives since we'd last met and yet suddenly nothing else in the world mattered.

I stayed a wonderful four days in the house with Chrissie until I felt fully rested and revived. We didn't go anywhere or really do anything, but just spent time together. I assumed that I wouldn't be able to stay forever, I didn't ask. I didn't even try to look at the employment page of the local press. Why I didn't was a mystery. I was welcome in the house and I was getting on very well with Chrissie. In fact things were really quite wonderful between us. So why did I feel the need to move on? Was it a case of not fully appreciating what you have until it's gone? Maybe I thought I had to return to Brisbane to make money, back to Dave and the paintings business. Adelaide was unfamiliar, and I knew Brisbane well, perhaps I wanted the familiarity of Queensland again?

We rose late on my fourth morning at about ten o'clock. Chrissie made ham and cheese toasted sandwiches for breakfast. It was a Thursday morning and I was setting off for

Sydney. Money wasn't discussed and I was too proud to admit that I had none, but Chrissie gave me ten dollars. She must have known. It would be enough to get me to Sydney at least, which I estimated by looking at my map was probably two or three hitchhiking days away. By now I could quite accurately judge how long it might take to hitchhike across a country, looking at the density of the conurbation, the size of the roads, and the likely traffic flow.

Our last night together had been one of our best and again I wondered why I was leaving. Chrissie was travelling to Sydney on the following Sunday so why on earth didn't I wait and travel with her? Was it a case of selfish pride? I packed my bag with my clean fresh clothes and at two o'clock I left Chrissie and Limosa Court, and caught a bus to the eastern Adelaide suburb of Stirling.

PORTLAND BAY

"Do you wanna come in here with me, Bob, out the rain?"

I stood by the busy main road watching the traffic pass me by, while the previous four days with Chrissie filled my thoughts completely. To my surprise I was quite relaxed about standing by the road again, it was easy and familiar, and I felt well fed and rested. But I couldn't help thinking I was heading in the wrong direction, both physically and metaphorically. What had I just left behind? I stood like an automaton for a while, rolling my right thumb around into the road, not fully concentrating. The high volume of traffic meant that I was soon picked up and within a few minutes I was sitting comfortably in the back of a large warm car and was conveyed ten miles before being dropped off again.

My next lift was not quite so comfortable. I sat in the open in the back of a Ute with a large Doberman dog which sat staring and growling at me intermittently for half an hour. It wasn't restrained in any way and so if it had wanted to find out just what any of my brown limbs tasted like I imagined I'd have to wrestle the damned thing to the metal floor of the Ute or leap overboard at whatever speed we were travelling at. I readied myself with one hand nervously gripping the top of a tent pole in case I had to whip it out in an instant and beat the snarling monster away from me. Apart from all this, it seemed to be quite a good lift! The Ute was driven at a rapid pace along fast flowing inner ring-roads around and through eastern Adelaide and I could tell that I was heading roughly east, where I needed to go. It could easily have been a nightmare to find my way around without this lift.

Clouds were gathering in an increasingly grey sky above and I was becoming quite cold and uncomfortable before my lift eventually came to an end. I climbed out of the Ute intact and unchewed, and the dog barked and growled madly as I thanked the driver. The fearsome thing actually looked quite sorry to see me go, or it could have been disappointment that it hadn't managed a bite. A wait of just ten minutes followed before I was picked up by a young man in a smart, clean VW Beetle and taken 30 miles to a place called Tailem Bend. I then had to make a decision whether to take the Dukes Highway which was just a few miles further on, or to start straight away on the coast road to the right, the Princes Highway. I chose the latter, and this was probably a mistake. The Dukes Highway would have taken me a more direct route roughly straight across the state of Victoria through Bendigo before reaching Wagga Wagga, Yass, Goulburn, and then onto Sydney. I was now risking getting caught up in Melbourne city where I didn't need to go. I was impatient and the Princes Highway was already there in front of me, so I took it.

I stood on a corner at Tailem Bend for twenty minutes before I was picked up in a tiny and very tired Morris van which was driven by a man who gave his name as Bob, and his friend who said his name was also Bob. Clearly they didn't want to give me their real names, for some reason. Perhaps they were on the run? The old van was very slow, and as we drove along I could see the circular *Smiths* speedometer in the centre of the dashboard rarely exceeded fifty miles an hour. I could just see through the glass window behind the seats that the back of the van was full of boxes, rolls of carpet and bits of furniture, but neither of them would elaborate as to what they were doing or where they were going. I was just glad of the lift and relieved to be out of the cold.

The change in temperature from further north was incredible, and it became very clear my biggest problem now might be insufficient warm clothing. I'd been in Brisbane for the last nine months and this was the furthest south I'd ever been on my hitchhiking adventure. I had no idea it could be this cool, and I was so very glad I'd brought my jeans. I would have been very cold standing around in a pair of brief cut-off jeans shorts all the time.

We drove past Mt. Gambier in the dark and continued on the Princes Highway into Victoria. It was ten o'clock at night when we passed Portland and it was in Portland Bay where it was decided we should stop for the night. We pulled over into a lay-by next to the road. There was very little traffic, we were miles from anywhere, and it was pitch dark. Why on earth did Bob and Bob decide to stop there? They were both physically bigger and stronger than me and it never once occurred to me even for a moment that I would come to any harm in their company.

One of the Bob's decided to sleep in the van lying across the front seats. There wasn't any room in the back of the van so the other Bob just lay down next to the vehicle. I thought this was very odd and doubted that he would get any sleep at all. It may have been okay if the weather was good and if we'd been a lot further north, but we weren't.

I pitched my tent by the road quite close to the van and the few tent pegs I had were not anchoring very well in the stodgy earth. It had clearly been raining recently, and quite a lot too, judging by the softness of the ground. I reached into my rucksack and ate a few slices of bread and jam Chrissie had given me and they tasted wonderful. I was still very hungry but I decided to leave the rest for another time. The onshore wind from the Southern Ocean only a few miles away was gaining in strength and I had barely crawled into my sleeping bag when I was alarmed by the sound of very heavy rain lashing down onto the tent. It had never been tested like this before. A mild tropical breeze and a slight desert wind was all it had known up until then. The wind shook the little tent and the rain fell very heavily, reminiscent of a desert flash flood, but this just wasn't abating, and if anything it was getting worse. I thought of the Bob lying down outside the van and took a look outside. Sure enough, there he was, in the leeward side of the van but clearly getting very wet.

"Do you wanna come in here with me, Bob, out the rain?" I shouted to him above the noise of the increasing storm. He stood up immediately and ran the few yards to the tent, clumsily shoving himself almost sideways through the small zip-up entrance. My temporary home was supposedly just a one man tent, so consequently it was then suddenly 100% over occupied. But the rain was truly awful and no-one should have been expected to stay outside in those conditions. We had to lie down together in a kind of spooning fashion in order to fit in and not bulge the sides out, and it was not very comfortable. We just managed to refrain from putting an arm around one another, even though it may have helped to save space. But this was the first time we'd slept together so I guess you shouldn't push it on a first date.

The wind and rain continued relentlessly, but the tent seemed to be holding up and for a while I thought we might actually get some sleep. Suddenly, and just as I was daring to dream of being elsewhere, two of the guy lines popped their pegs simultaneously and the whole tent collapsed. At least it would have collapsed had it not been for the human contents inside who were now sitting up and trying to make sense of what was happening. I managed to wriggle free first, crawling out the zip front as though escaping from an enormous wet paper bag. When I turned to stand upright the rain hit me ruthlessly full in the face and I was soaked in an instant. Bob followed, catching his feet on the tent and partially dragging it around the lay-by as a result. I had to hop about and stamp on one corner to stop it from escaping. The two of us then stood in the horizontal driving rain trying to gain what shelter we could from something that was flapping and blowing about like a large, uncontrollable wet flag.

After what seemed hours but was probably only a few desperate minutes we managed to get it pitched again and we clambered back inside. It held together quite well for a while and just as we began to believe we might have beaten the elements we realised to our horror and with some resigned disappointment that it was starting to fill up with water. The tent was flooding, and it was getting worse. I initially tried bailing the water out with my hands as though I was in a sinking lifeboat but it was a hopeless task. Just then as I was busy pointlessly bailing, the tent popped the same guy lines again and collapsed on top of us. The wet nylon tent smothered us both and stuck to us like cling-film.

At the time it was just too stupid and nightmarish to be funny. There just wasn't anything amusing about it despite the fact we both probably looked like *Laurel & Hardy* in some ridiculous slapstick camping episode, mainly because I was quite tall and thin and Bob was round and portly. In the total darkness and heavy rain we managed to pitch the damned thing again, only to have it blow down once more after only ten minutes. We both persisted with some admirable determination but it continued to defy us and blew down *four more times* despite our best efforts. On each occasion we became wetter and ever more miserable and despondent. Where was the other Bob during all this? Was he fast asleep in the van?

I grabbed my rucksack which had thankfully remained remarkably dry, and then Bob and I opened the passenger door to the van and climbed in without giving the dry Bob any choice in the matter. Bob should have locked it if he didn't want to be invaded by two cold, very wet and angry bodies. The three of us sat in the car side by side and tried to get some sleep sitting up, two of us in wet clothes right through to our underwear. It was a peculiarly and uniquely miserable experience. The rain and wind continued and the fate of the tent was unknown; I had long since passed caring.

Light came eventually and for a while the rain actually stopped. I climbed out of the van and searched for my tent. I found it ten yards away hanging in a tree as though it had been blown up there by a hurricane or a powerful bomb. Luckily by some miracle because my rucksack was hardly wet most of the contents including my diary were dry. I gathered up the tent as best I could and rolled it up like an enormous sopping dishcloth. I felt very cold, extremely hungry and incredibly miserable. My underpants were very wet and as I moved around my boots were sodden so they squelched quite loudly as I walked. My hands and feet were particularly cold. I wondered for a moment why on earth I'd left Chrissie in Adelaide and I felt sick with remorse.

You know those awful occasions when you've been camping and it hasn't really worked out, when you try to put on a brave face but you seriously question your own sanity for being there in the first place? This was one of the best examples of such deep camping regret. I was still only a day away from Chrissie and I wanted to abandon everything and run back to her.

I stood close up to the van and put on some relatively dry socks, dry underpants, a dry t-shirt which did have a couple of wet patches in it actually, and despite the cool weather, my jeans shorts. I rolled up my wet jeans and my other clothes and stuffed them into my rucksack. I sealed my precious diary in a plastic bag that I took from the van to protect it from damp. I took out some of the sliced brown bread Chrissie had given me which was also in a plastic bag and I gave the Bobs a few slices each which they ate with some of the melon and pineapple jam. We had a reasonable breakfast but I would have killed for a long hot drink of some sort.

After a quick piss by the road we were ready to set off. The warmth and the motion of the vehicle had an instantly soporific effect on me and I slept on and off for most of the journey. Just after Warrnambool we forked left and stayed on the Princes Highway. I realised that according to my map I'd just missed seeing The Twelve Apostles on the Great Ocean Road, a spectacular series of rock formations on the beach. It was yet another place to add to my 'almost seen' list of places.

Despite the leisurely pace of the old Morris we reached the town of Geelong in the late morning. It was still dull and overcast, but at least it was not raining when I had to climb out of the lovely warm womb the little van had become. My feet were quite wet again from being inside my sodden boots, but other than that I was okay. The name Geelong suddenly seemed strangely familiar to me, so I opened my rucksack to find my address book. Sure enough, in amongst the mildly damp pages was the name and address of another friend who I'd known from my early kibbutz days.

MELBOURNE

Apple-bobbing

Abandoned by the Bobs in the centre of Geelong I saw the road signs that pointed north east for Melbourne. I stopped in a café by the main road and bought a large, sweet milky coffee, which was wonderful. I rolled one of my last cigarettes and felt completely revived afterwards. I sat staring at Val's address in my open address book for several agonising minutes before deciding not to contact her. Val may not even have been there, but more importantly, I didn't know her very well and it would have looked obvious as to why I was visiting. My connection with her was tenuous at best, having merely worked a few shifts on the zipper in the kibbutz factory several years before.

I spent half an hour in the café before I resumed hitching. After only ten minutes a well-dressed old man with thick grey hair picked me up in an immaculate Commodore saloon and took me halfway to Melbourne. He was very apologetic when he realised he would have to leave me by the road when it had just started raining, because he could no doubt see that I wasn't dressed for bad weather. But I didn't want to stay at Werribee in Port Philip Bay, even if it did look like quite a nice place.

I then stood for a while under the cover of a bus shelter until I realised buses were pulling over and stopping for me but cars were not. Never hitchhike while standing at a bus stop! After twenty minutes in the rain under the relative cover of a gum tree I was picked up by a British ex-pat in a VW van. We both agreed how sad English people were for staying in poor old England and not making the leap to live in the warm Australian sun. I realised the obvious irony in the conversation as I'd just been standing shivering in heavy rain and in a particularly cold wind.

My lift dropped me on the outskirts of Melbourne. I could see the tall buildings of the central business district in the distance, but I had no real need to get any closer. My last lift had pointed out where I could find the start of Highway 31 which would take me to Sydney. I walked for a few minutes to find the right spot and quite quickly a man in a large high-sided van pulled up and took me 6 miles or 10 kilometres around Melbourne city, much closer to Highway 31.

Ten minutes later I was standing near the start of the highway and half an hour passed before I was picked up. Half an hour doesn't sound a long time and it wasn't by outback standards. But this was one of the main highways linking two of Australia's biggest cities, so I must have been passed by thousands of vehicles. It was a good job none of these people were driving up north or no-one would ever get a lift. Unless it was a case of 'someone will give him a lift, but not me…' Up north with relatively few vehicles on the remote roads, each driver was forced to search his or her own conscience that little bit deeper, knowing the hitchhiker would be standing there alone in the heat probably for several hours.

My lift was quite a good-looking woman in her early forties with long, thick, black hair which tumbled down beyond her shoulders, and who had a very strange accent that seemed to be a mixture of North American and Aussie drawl. She stopped talking only when drawing breath to speak and she drove her car, which was some sort of expensive sports coupe, as though she was late for her own funeral. I didn't mind though. The countryside flashed past, there was some decent country and western music on the stereo, and the ride was warm and luxurious. There was a very strong smell of freshly cut flowers and when I noticed there weren't any visible I realised it was her perfume fragrance that had completely filled the car. No doubt I didn't smell too good so hopefully she may not have noticed my own malodorous whiff as I sat next to her. She was positioned quite low down in her seat and I could see from this that she wasn't very tall but she was reasonably slim and very feminine. She was wearing a tight black dress which was cut surprisingly low across her very generous chest. Her large, heaving bosoms therefore bounced around very interestingly, like two bald men apple-bobbing and she was gripping the gear stick with her left hand in a very provocative manner. But that could just have been my imagination or even some wishful thinking. Strange things can flash through your mind sometimes when hitchhiking.

On closer observation my lift was clearly a very sexy woman and was obviously quite wealthy. It occurred to me just for an instant that I could abandon everything and stay with this woman if she wanted me to, even if she was probably twice my age. I could be her driver, her handyman, and concubine. I could turn my hand to anything she wanted, within reason. Anything. She kept talking effusively about equal sexual rights between men and women, and even how men and women had the right to have sex with equal rights. I just kept nodding in agreement and admiring the view, both on the inside and the outside of the car. It wasn't until the lift was sadly over and my daydreaming had ended that I really thought about what she'd been saying. She really did seem quite reluctant to let me out of the car.

I stood by the roadside in Benalla with sweet perfume smells still in my nostrils and wonderful images of bald men apple-bobbing. The weather had improved and it wasn't quite so cold. I was now on the same road I would have been had I not made the disastrous detour around the coast road and past Melbourne. It seemed I'd wasted at least twenty four hours in some of the worst weather I'd ever experienced in Australia. It was late afternoon and I was getting hungry. I thought I'd make a little more progress on the journey before stopping for food, so I wanted one more lift just a few more miles. The urge to get a good lift sometimes became intoxicating; almost like trying to catch that elusive great wave, the special one that would carry you right up the beach. If I stopped now I might miss that lift, the one that would take me all the way.

Almost an hour passed until a middle-aged Canadian couple in a rented saloon took me to Wangaratta, the neighbouring town to Glenrowan, where the infamous outlaw bushranger Ned Kelly made his last stand. He was captured there and eventually hanged in Melbourne Gaol in 1880. Wangaratta seemed like a very nice town and as it was growing dark I decided to pitch my tent for the night. I couldn't find a campsite so I set up the tent on some soft grass by the road, near to a hotel. I had to double up on tent pegs as some were missing, no doubt lost in the great Portland Bay camping disaster, and two guy lines had to be fixed to a nearby tree. I also used some branches of the tree to hang up my wet clothes and my sleeping bag, which had all been crunched up in one damp lump in the bottom of my rucksack since early that morning. Once I'd pitched the tent I ate some of the last of my bread and jam for dinner. I left one slice for the morning. I then smartened myself up as best I could and walked calmly with my rucksack into the nearby hotel via the main entrance and straight to the nearest toilets.

I used the toilet facilities, washed myself as best I could and brushed my teeth. The hotel was plush and warm with soft elevator music playing throughout the ground floor. The sinks were spotlessly clean and the chrome-plated taps twinkled like stars in the bright spotlights above the wall mirrors. I wanted to leave the tent for a while to dry if possible, because it was still very wet inside, and as a result it had acquired that awful unpleasant stale damp smell. I walked out of the toilets and then dared to sit in a luxurious leather chair in the hotel foyer for over an hour, reading the day's newspapers and writing in my diary before eventually returning to my tent.

It was completely dark when I climbed inside my tent and I was disappointed to find it was still very damp. My sleeping bag was also quite moist, but I had no choice but to make the best of it and climb inside. This very damp night was just a continuation of the low point of my trip which started in the rain the night before. I didn't have any extra clothes to put on, they were all hanging in the tree above me, but luckily it was not a cold night, and I managed a few hours of relatively good sleep, considering the conditions. I began to think that I might be able to sleep anywhere, even hanging from a washing line, which you can if you are tired enough.

I woke up just before dawn. I was again very cold and hungry. The damp had penetrated my dry clothing and I needed warmth quickly. I saw some activity at the hotel so I left the tent pitched and walked into the front foyer and bought a large milky coffee which I loaded with sugar as usual. It was clear by then that I wasn't a resident, as few of them were up at that time, but the staff didn't seem to mind. My core temperature rose immediately as did my spirits and I returned to the tent for breakfast. I ate my last slice of bread and jam after which I realised all my food had gone again.

My clothes had dried quite well in the night but still not enough to wear comfortably. I checked each item in turn and left them out to dry as long as I possibly could. I must have looked very odd in the daylight, standing as I was not far from the main road at my little tent wearing skimpy jeans shorts, with all my clothes dangling from the tree above me. It is a credit to the Aussies and their generally laid back approach to life that no-one came up to me to ask who I was and what I was doing.

I de-pitched my tent and started thumbing at about seven o'clock. Almost immediately I was picked up by a dark-skinned white man who gave his name as Frank. He told me he was Majorcan by birth and had lived in Australia for the last sixteen years, hence his very broad Aussie accent. I began to notice that a lot of visible ethnic minorities in Australia had the broadest Australian accents. They had probably developed them deliberately in an effort to fit in, as indeed I had done. I recounted several happy family holidays in Majorca and Frank seemed very pleased to be reminiscing about his homeland. He was driving a very smart Subaru Ute which had a tremendous rate of acceleration, so he seemed to be doing very well for himself. I recovered my morale and Frank gave me some biscuits he had in his car and which tasted wonderful.

The beautiful rolling green countryside of northern Victoria became New South Wales when we crossed over the wide and resplendent Murray River. I couldn't enjoy the view and the ride to the full because for the first time in days I really needed a toilet, and not just for a piss. I didn't feel able or willing to ask my driver to stop somewhere so I managed to hold it and suffer in silence.

We passed through Yass and Goulburn, just skimming past Canberra and the ACT, the Australian Capital Territory, before I was finally dropped off at Campbelltown, between Wollongong and Sydney. I'd been with Frank in his Subaru Ute for five hours, and it had been a wonderful lift. Frank had been interesting company and probably realised I was tired as he allowed me to sleep undisturbed for long periods. As the Subaru sped away I found the nearest pub and hobbled into the toilets. It was quite a few minutes before I emerged again at least several pounds lighter and much happier. It seems the sudden absence of a baked bean diet had caused a firm blockage in my system, which I don't mind admitting took some shifting. Anyone listening to me suffering would have thought I was probably giving birth. It reminded me of the old Elvis joke: he had all those number ones but in the end it was a number two that killed him.

I decided to have a walk around Campbelltown, and just out of curiosity I stepped inside the railway station. To my great surprise I saw that the fares to Sydney were very reasonable. I double-checked my finances and it seemed I could actually afford a train ticket to Sydney. I had to be sure about what I was doing because this would take up every last penny. I had friends in Sydney and the following day was Sunday, when Chrissie was due to arrive and meet me, so I should be okay just as long as I could get there.

I was extremely hungry and I wanted to get to Sydney as quickly as possible, so I made my decision and bought a ticket with only a few cents remaining. Now with no money for food or drink I feasted on tap water in the station toilets. I filled my water bottle and used the final remnants of tobacco in my pocket to make one last cigarette, while waiting for the train.

The steel double-deck train was sleek and shiny with

brightly coloured upholstery and lots of moulded plastic. Like many similar things in Australia there was plenty of room and it was clean and tidy. It accelerated smoothly and swayed very gently along the track, and I found a quiet seat where I fell asleep very quickly. I had pleasant dreams of warm sunny beaches, large chicken and mushroom pizzas and a wonderful happy return to Sydney.

SYDNEY, AGAIN

"I'll see you again soon, right?"

The train terminated at a very busy Circular Quay. It was Saturday afternoon and everywhere in sight was thronged with tourists. Sydney seemed familiar if a little frightening too, like a pleasant but very annoying older cousin who would bully you at every opportunity. I didn't have enough money for a ferry or a bus so I made my way up to the Harbour Bridge and started walking across it. Yet again I found myself trudging this route in the same lamentable manner, with nothing in my pockets. When I finally arrived at my friend's address in Premier Street, Neutral Bay there was no reply to knocking, so I sat down outside and waited. I'd become quite an expert at waiting, whether it was standing up or sitting down, I could do both equally as well. I assumed they still lived there; or rather it was a case of *hoping* someone was still there who I knew.

After an hour's increasingly anxious wait when my fingernails were nervously bitten down in the absence of anything to smoke, Mick arrived home. Mick was one of my friend's flat mates I'd met on a few previous occasions, so he opened the door and we both entered the flat together. I dumped my rucksack in the kitchen and took a shower. Mick made me a wonderful sandwich and a coffee, for which I was very grateful. I washed my clothes in the kitchen sink with some proper washing powder, and then stepped outside the back door. The weather was fine and warm with a light afternoon breeze so they wouldn't take long to dry. Standing at the washing line in the back garden I was reminded of the fantastic view of the harbour and the bridge, which was actually quite spectacular, particularly at night.

My friends Anne and Phil arrived home and when Anne saw me she just shouted with obvious surprise:

"What are *you* doing heeere? I thought you were up north somewhere?!" to which I simply shrugged my shoulders and mumbled a few lines to the effect that it hadn't quite worked out. I assumed they were talking about Brisbane because I don't remember telling them anything about my Darwin trip. My friends were thankfully very sympathetic and my staying there didn't seem to be an issue. I was given the immediate use of the sofa in the lounge room on which I could sleep. Anne cooked a wonderful meal and I remember the evening movie on the television was the brilliant Peter Sellers in *The Pink Panther Strikes Again*. I could breathe a sigh of relief in that I was again safe in a home environment, even if it was only temporary.

In the morning after breakfast I headed out quite early to walk back to Circular Quay. My original arrangement with Chrissie was that we would meet at midday down at the quay. I was excited at the prospect of seeing her again but my circumstances couldn't have been worse. I was still broke and would be relying on her for money. This was denting my pride and making a difficult situation almost intolerable. It would influence events for many years to come.

Chrissie looked wonderful as she emerged from the crowd and we kissed and embraced. Suddenly Sydney appeared warm and sunny again, with delicate wisps of fair weather cumulus floating across a beautiful deep blue sky. She seemed as pleased to see me as I was to see her, with broad smiles and some anxious mutual hand-holding. We walked around the quay for a while and out to the opera house. We talked as we leaned on the railings overlooking the harbour with the huge shell-like roof structures of the opera house behind us. Ferries came and went churning up the clean blue water, and groups of oriental tourists noisily gathered near the steps shoving one another around to get the best pictures.

Chrissie and I took a ferry back across to Neutral Bay and walked up the hill to Premier Street. Phil answered the door and ushered us inside. The three of us chatted for a while and Phil made coffee. We sat down at the kitchen table and I scanned a copy of the *Sydney Morning Herald* for the employment section. If only I could get a job, I'd be able to stay. How could I stay indefinitely without one? Whatever job it was it would have to be for cash-in-hand, as without a work permit I couldn't take up any decent, formal employment. I couldn't see any ads for *Décor Galleries* or anything remotely similar. Perhaps they no longer existed.

After a couple of hours we crossed the water again and returned to Circular Quay. We walked up to The Rocks area and found a pub. I was subsisting on Chrissie's charity and I was very conscious of it and felt acutely embarrassed. This was not part of my plan.

We met one of Chrissie's friends, Diana, and a Swiss guy called Peter, and we drank more beer together. Chrissie and I then returned to Neutral Bay where we slept quite uncomfortably together on the sofa. It was not the best of arrangements and in the morning when I woke up I realised that I'd already made my decision to leave Sydney and return to Brisbane. I didn't even want to try looking for work again in Sydney. At least I knew Dave was up there in Brisbane where there was a strong possibility of making some money. I could return to the flat in East Brisbane and take up where I'd left off. I didn't think I'd have to do this, as I'd honestly hoped that somewhere else in that vast country would be where I'd find my fortune, but clearly it wasn't to be. Maybe I could return to Sydney and Chrissie at a later date, but with some money in my pockets? I just knew I couldn't stay there in such circumstances, my pride wouldn't allow it. Was I being foolish, or was it the right thing to do?

The next morning I looked into Chrissie's deep blue eyes and held her hands tightly as we said goodbye to each other. It wasn't meant to be for very long, a few weeks maybe, or a couple of months. It seemed we loved each other and we wanted to be together, but circumstances were just too difficult.

"Babe, things will be okay... I love you, and I'll see you again soon, right?" Chrissie said as she smiled and held onto my hands. With money that Chrissie had given me I bought a train ticket to Hornsby, one of Sydney's most northern suburbs, from where I could start hitching. A dark wave of panic swept over me and I thought that my heart might burst in my chest. I had a sudden fear that I might never see Chrissie again, and after all our previous parting moments this would finally be the last time. It just shook me like an icy blast right through to my bones as our hands separated and the ugly distance in time and space between us began to grow immediately. Surely things would work out as Chrissie said, and we would be back in each other's arms in no time? I tried to push the situation to the back of my mind, and I know I was able to draw on some of the cold-hearted determination that I'd acquired in the previous few months as I turned my back and walked away.

I had my first lift in the cab of a road train when I was just a few miles north of Sydney, which took me to the next town up the coast, Newcastle. It was ironic that I was given such a lift on the busy roads near Sydney when so many similar vehicles had passed me by in the outback without stopping. Everything about the road train was enormous, including the driver. He was taking his huge vehicle to Port Hunter in Newcastle to be loaded for a long trip north. A CB radio hung from the centre of the dashboard and it crackled and chattered away incessantly. The driver was keen to make conversation with me but I was preoccupied with thoughts of Chrissie. I was determined to return with full pockets one day very soon, and maybe then we could carry on our lives together. Did we have a future? We'd never yet had any cross words or an argument of any kind, and whenever we met we seemed to carry on just where we'd left off, regardless of the time between meetings.

It took me a while to get out of Newcastle. I walked for several miles to get as close as I could to the most northern suburbs and when a lift came I was very lucky. The driver was going up to the Gold Coast just south of Brisbane and was happy to take me all the way there. This would be another brilliant lift of about 350 miles, or 600 kilometres. My driver was a middle-aged man with greasy black hair and a pot-belly, and he drove at high speed almost all the time. He kept looking across at me and smiling broadly in a very friendly manner as he talked. He smoked and left the packet open on the centre console insisting I help myself whenever I wanted, which I did. This seemed to please him and he then kept asking whether there was anything else he could do for me. I thought this was a rather peculiar thing to say and so I told him I was happy just with the lift, thanks very much.

Darkness fell on the Pacific Highway when we were between Port Macquarie and Coffs Harbour. My driver showed no signs of wanting to stop other than very briefly for fuel. I was happy with this; it was a good lift, so we pressed on.

We passed through Grafton and then Ballina, roaring on through both towns without stopping and it was at this point that my driver suddenly asked me a direct question, which came across as being more like a peremptory order.

"You'll stay with me, in my room tonight, eh?" he said, as I could sense his head was turned around towards me in the darkness of the car and I could feel his eyes looking at me. I daren't turn my head to see his face. I didn't quite know what to say, or what to do. I'd spent the night in motel rooms with drivers before and there hadn't been a problem. But I sensed something about this man that I just wasn't happy about. It could have been hitchhiker's intuition, or just plain common sense, but the vibes were quite strange from this bloke.

"No it's okay mate, I've got me tent here you know…" I replied in my best Aussie accent, tapping my rucksack on the floor and the tent poles sticking out the top.

"No I insist you stay with me in my room. It would be nice…"

"No, really, I've got my tent, thanks all the same…"

"We could have some beers in the bar and then go up to the room. You'd be okay, we could just have a drink and have some fun that's all, okay?" and there was some firmness in the man's voice edged with a slight touch of pleading. I tried to maintain an air of disinterest but I was becoming quite worried. The man was physically much bigger in stature than I was and I suddenly noticed the sheer size of his enormous hands, in addition to his very thick and extremely hairy arms. I was thin, with long brown legs which were quite slender in my brief jeans shorts and no doubt I looked like I had narrow hips too, like a Spanish waiter, so maybe the man fancied his chances? Should I have felt flattered or worried, or both? I began to feel very uneasy as the car bounded along the dark road, and felt some irony in the fact that I was almost back in Brisbane and hadn't once felt uncomfortable with a driver during all those thousands of miles until that moment.

I tried to keep the conversation as light as possible but my lift kept repeating his offer of a room and was becoming ever more insistent. When we eventually arrived in the brightly lit streets of Surfer's Paradise I elected to get out of the car as soon as I could. Despite the fact it was one-thirty in the morning the main street of Surfers was busy with people and giving my driver little option I opened the door at traffic lights and literally bailed out onto the road as if the car was about to explode. Remembering my manners I shouted back "Thanks for the lift!" but the man didn't reply and drove away at speed.

I trudged through Surfers for half an hour and eventually found a quiet area of firm sand just off the road to pitch my tent. Surfers and the rest of the Gold Coast was very impressive, like Las Vegas by the sea, with jostling lines of skyscraper hotels and apartments close to the wonderful clean beaches, and it was clear judging by all the construction work that it was becoming much bigger all the time. This was no surprise, the beach at Surfers is probably the best in the world and the ocean is warm and safe, with lifeguards patrolling all the popular areas.

I slept very well until after dawn when I realised I'd pitched my tent very close to a busy thoroughfare. But no-one was really bothered, just as they hadn't been anywhere else in Australia. People seemed genuinely unconcerned and didn't see my little tent as any kind of problem. I packed away quickly and headed off towards the main highway again. I was now so close I was getting impatient and just wanted to get there. Traffic between the Gold Coast and Brisbane was very heavy. In two excellent lifts I was back in East Brisbane and walking towards the flat. I'd been away for weeks and had no idea what I might find, if indeed anyone was still there. I sincerely hoped someone would be, because as usual I was broke and very hungry.

BACK IN BRISBANE

Sean, Pat, and Anika

I climbed the back steps onto the fourth floor landing and knocked on the door of the flat. No-one answered. I knocked again, much louder this time. It was eleven o'clock in the morning. I hoped that if the flat was still occupied by people I knew then it would be quiet and calm, somewhere for me to take stock of my life and to make some plans for my eventual return to Sydney. Maybe Rob was still there, and Karl, and Jane too no doubt. The four of us would get on well again and everything would work out.

To my relief, the door was opened by Rob, who was barefoot, deeply tanned, and wearing a thin and brightly coloured sarong tied casually around his waist. He looked as though he should have been wandering the streets of Bali rather than Brisbane. His hair was ruffled and he squinted at me as though he'd just woken up, which he clearly had. The flat appeared dark and smelt musty inside, like an antique shop or an old people's home, and I could see bodies on the floor and figures wandering about, smoking. Who on earth were all these people?

"Jonathan! Hi! You're back! Come on in mate, good to see you! There's some people here I think you might know!" and Rob virtually dragged me quite firmly by the arm into the flat. As I stepped inside the figures on the floor stood up and wandered over to me. It was Sean, Anika, and Pat. I was extremely shocked to see them in the flat. It seemed that while I was away my three friends had arrived from Europe, keen to exploit the wonderful life I had so keenly described to them in all my stoned letters from months before. They'd come to see if the Australian streets really were paved with gold as I'd described countless times in my writing. I had no way of knowing they were even planning to come over, let alone that they had actually arrived, due to the fact that I had not been contactable while wandering about the country.

Sean was my Irish mate I'd met while working in Germany along with Pat, our mutual friend, and Anika, the Dutch girl from the kibbutz who was now Sean's girlfriend. As if this wasn't quite enough people crammed into the place, Rob introduced me to Karen, his girlfriend, and Ann, Karl's girlfriend. Karl was still there, as was Jane, and all eight people were living almost literally on top of one another in the two bedroomed flat, which now seemed extremely cramped. I thought of the time Rich and I had lived there, just the two of us, and it now looked like an entirely different place.

I was surprised but pleased to see my friends, though it was clear they had travelled ten thousand miles from Europe largely because of all those weird letters I'd sent encouraging them to come over, insisting it was a wonderful place and how easy it was to make pots of money. How could I now tell them that I was hungry and broke, and that most of those letters were written when I was bombed off my tits on weed and were quite unrealistic? I felt terribly guilty about it all and didn't have the heart to be completely honest, at least not straight away. I also felt obliged to help them out, even though clearly I was not in any position to offer assistance because I was in dire need of it myself.

My immediate problem was quickly resolved when I was given food and then beer with a cigarette. I sat with Sean, Pat and Anika and we laughed and joked about how they had arrived in Australia. Sean admitted that my letters had been the main prompt but he also stated he was fully aware they must have been written when I was intoxicated, stoned most likely. I felt a little less guilty after this but I knew that I needed to see Dave as soon as I could and set myself up at selling paintings again and making some money, if possible. It seemed that Sean, Anika and Pat had only just arrived a few days before and hadn't started looking for work yet. I thought I'd ask Dave if he'd take them all on at the paintings business, as I really did believe they would be good at it. As I looked around the crowded flat my thoughts drifted for a moment back to the emptiness of the Australian outback, and I then wondered what had been the purpose of my great trek across the country if I was right back where I'd started.

Dave found out that I was back in Brisbane and came around to the flat the next morning. He was tanned and smart in a clean, pressed shirt and slacks, and didn't immediately offer me the opportunity to return to the company. I had left with the probable intention of never returning, but now I was back, and with some additional mouths to feed. Dave was clearly enjoying being the centre of attention and it was only after meeting Sean and engaging with him in a very lively conversation that it seemed there was indeed a chance we were all to be offered a job. It was with a huge sense of relief therefore that we started the next night.

I was given a car and a supervisor's role, along with Rob. Dave performed the 'rave' showing us all how to sell the paintings, and then we were off, out into the better suburbs of Brisbane. I took Sean, Pat, and Anika and kept trying to remind them how to sell the paintings, even though I suddenly realised my own sales abilities had completely expired by that time. No amount of scotch beforehand could bring me to a doorstep again; I hated the very idea of it, but I decided to keep this to myself. I needed money but something inexplicable had happened to me on my great hitchhiking trip that brought this whole caper into irrelevance. I felt unable to do it anymore because there was something about it that was unpleasant in the extreme, and I couldn't overcome this feeling. You occasionally find this happens in life, when you have a particularly wonderful and thought-provoking experience, after which many previous past times or aspects of your life can then seem strangely empty and ridiculous, like post-holiday blues but hugely amplified. I knew that if I tried selling that awful rubbish door-to-door again I would feel like Sisyphus, condemned to roll a huge boulder up a hill only to watch it roll back down and to repeat this pointlessness forever.

On their first night a few good sales were made between Sean, Pat, and Anika, but they didn't sell for much of a profit margin and so they hardly made any money for themselves. The only person to make money was Dave, as usual. They tried the next night and every night for a week but they were not having much success. They had the occasional flurry as in any sales-based occupation, but these were rare and between long periods of poor sales and barren nights. On one occasion Sean and I had a very acrimonious argument about where I was supposed to pick them up and this soured our relationship, already strained from the poor sales. I was genuinely surprised they couldn't sell more, I'd been quite sure with Sean's often ebullient and friendly personality he would be very successful.

With nine people now living in the flat a move was necessitated and organised mainly by Rob and his girlfriend Karen. They found a large, old, wooden Queenslander house on Main Avenue, Coorparoo, a suburb a few miles away, and with virtually no possessions all nine of us moved into it very quickly in one afternoon. Sadly the bond on the flat was not returned to me because on the night of the infamous naked party I very stupidly used an aerosol as a flamethrower to kill a cockroach and it had burned a hole in the living room carpet. I could have really benefited from that money too. Perhaps when I left weeks before I should have demanded the bond money from Rob, but then I wouldn't have been able to claim residence back there as I did.

Sean, Pat, Anika and I automatically followed Rob and Karen to the house at Coorparoo, assuming that we were also invited to live there. It seemed Rob probably didn't have the heart to tell us otherwise, or else he may have done so. Our lowly status in the house was clear however, as the four of us lived like refugees by simply lying on the floor in corners of the dining area and lounge room, while the Kiwis lived in the bedrooms, and slept in the beds. Even Jane had her own room.

Occasionally an old friend from kibbutz days who lived in

Brisbane, Gareth, would visit us with his friend Ronald, and they would bring with them a small piece of hash which we would sit around and eagerly devour between us. On one such very hot afternoon we tried to watch *Star Wars* on the TV which was 'simulcast' with a local radio station *FM 104*. We then fed the sound through the stereo and it should have been great but the TV picture kept blanking out at crucial moments and in particular when the music suddenly went very loud, which was usually when Darth Vader made an appearance. The television would very annoyingly switch itself off for a few moments, so we never actually saw what he did to people and why he was supposed to be so evil. As a consequence almost every time Darth Vader stomped into view he was booed very loudly by us, not because he was an evil character but because of what he seemed to be doing to our television. You can imagine the consequences for the story and it made the whole thing quite hilarious if virtually unwatchable.

I sent one of my diaries home to my parents in England for safe-keeping, and bought another blank diary. I started writing in it avidly, filling several pages every day with my activities – or lack of them – in Brisbane at the time. But I also wrote in great detail of my trip around Australia, perhaps as a means of escape from my current circumstances. I was acutely aware of being surrounded by people with no means of escape, even for a few days.

After weeks of solitude and living simply with my own thoughts while hitchhiking it was something of a shock to be in a house that was so crowded. After a week it finally became clear to me that my friends were never going to be successful at selling paintings. There were some rancorous arguments on occasions between us, which only prompted me further to seek a way out if possible. Things seemed to be deteriorating rapidly.

THE STORY BRIDGE

"No, we're fine officer, thanks..."

There were some other lighter moments to life in Coorparoo. One of the benefits of living on Main Avenue was our close proximity to an open-air, public swimming pool, just across the road. It wasn't actually directly across the road, but it was if you climbed over the fence and bunked in for nothing at night. It was a wonderful full-size Olympic pool and though it was probably not heated it was almost always warm. There was a diving board at one end and as usual when we were drunk it seemed a great idea to go for a free swim in the dark.

I had never jumped off anything as high as a diving board in complete darkness before. It was an unusual and a thrilling experience, leaping through the air not quite knowing how far the water was below you while falling. It was also highly amusing and with all the laughter and loud splashing it wasn't long before the pool attendant who lived in a house on site would come charging out of his front door waving his fists and threatening to call the police. Sean, Pat and I would then quickly hurl ourselves back over the six-foot fence and across the road to safety. Even in the daytime entry to the pool was only a few dollars, so it was pure luxury to have it on our doorstep, and our swimming improved tremendously as a result. We once had to spend a whole day by the pool in an enforced exile when the landlord of the house was due to call around to collect some of his property. There should have been four people in residence and not nine, so we had to make ourselves scarce. At least that was the reason Rob gave for wanting to be rid of us for the day.

Gareth called around on one occasion in his parent's four-by-four and took us on a sight-seeing trip to Mount Glorious, a fantastic rain forest national park west of Brisbane. It was an area of real tropical jungle with dense undergrowth, cool mountain streams and beautiful exotic birds everywhere just like in the movies. To add to the realism I acquired a leech on my right ankle which I removed by branding it stereotypically with a lighted cigarette. All very dramatic but apparently it would have detached itself quite easily without having to resort to such Hollywood tactics. We heard bell birds and kookaburras and the forest was loud with the wondrous din of tropical life. It was great to get out of the house and see some of the Australian countryside again.

Later that night I found a few precious moments alone in the kitchen and sat down at the table. I could hear Pink Floyd's *Dark Side of the Moon* album being played in the lounge room and the familiar lyrics and melodies drifted in through the open doorway. I remembered some of the other times I'd listened to it, better times, and I also remembered earlier that day standing at the top of a high waterfall gazing down at the water below. I wondered what it would have been like to jump. I could see myself falling thirty feet head-first, not into water, but onto the rocks. I could see my head smashing open like a water melon and my brains spilling out and splashing all across the rocks.

I reminded myself of my plan to find work, a proper job, and make some regular money. I bought a newspaper and applied for a post in a bank in central Brisbane. I'd hated the year I'd wasted working at the bank in Grantham, and I was acutely aware that I'd also failed at the bank interview in Darwin, but I had to give it a try, it was the only thing I knew. If only I could establish myself in a decent nine-to-five job, who knows where it would take me? I'd forgotten all about the stark and unavoidable fact that I was still an illegal immigrant, but I decided I'd wait and see if I was offered the job first before I worried about that minor technical issue. I completed a rather tiresome application form and submitted it with quite high hopes. Their response was eagerly awaited.

Dave called around to the house most nights after work. Sometimes he'd take me out for a drive in his car and we'd listen to Jean Michel Jarre's *Oxygene* and *Equinoxe* albums on the car stereo as usual. It was very atmospheric during the heavy rains and thunderstorms in Brisbane at that time of year, tearing around the city's wide freeway streets at high speed and in luxurious comfort. We'd drive to the empty office and smoke while silently playing some highly competitive games of backgammon. Dave was proud of the fact that he had taught me how to play the game, and took great pleasure in beating me every time, until recently. I could beat him almost whenever I wanted to now, and this was a source of annoyance to Dave. He was clearly a man who wanted everything his own way.

It was on one such night when Dave and I returned to the house quite late when someone made a ridiculous suggestion which everyone seemed to think was a good idea at the time.

"Let's climb the Story Bridge!" someone said. It was unclear who made this suggestion but within a few minutes Dave was driving me, Rob, Karl and Sean down towards the river in the centre of Brisbane. The Story Bridge is an iconic structure in Brisbane, though obviously not as famous as the bridge across Sydney harbour. It's not as aesthetically pleasing or quite as large either, but it is a formidable steel structure that stands a couple of hundred feet above the Brisbane River, with a wide roadway running across it.

By this time it was very late at night and we parked the car near the end of the bridge and walked to one side of the roadway. In between passing cars we took hold of the grey steel girders and began to climb. Sadly, or luckily for us, there were gates preventing high access but it was possible to reach the level girders which crossed over the roadway. We each selected one and edged our way across, at least thirty feet above the road. Each girder was scarcely a foot wide and it wasn't until halfway across, at the point of no return, that I realised just how stupid I was. We must have been clearly visible to motorists passing by underneath us, like a drunken and much uglier version of the Von Trapp children dangling from the trees.

There was a real chance one or more of us could have quite easily fallen to our deaths from the bridge that night. We'd all been drinking and smoking and it was just the sort of stupid stunt you hear about that ends in disaster. Initial high-spirited laughing and joking evaporated away very quickly and each of us became extremely grateful to reach the other side and climb down onto the roadway in one piece. We walked together back towards Dave's car in a far more subdued mood than when we'd arrived.

Just as we left the bridge in search of the car a marked police vehicle pulled up and two uniformed male cops immediately jumped out. They came over to us and began asking questions.

"What have you blokes been doing here?" one of them asked in a very serious tone. There was an awkward and very embarrassing silence before the cops were given a round of dumb expressions and Gallic shrugs like guilty schoolboys to a teacher before someone said:

"Nothing, why?" I looked at Dave and realised to my horror in the bright light from the neon street lamps that we were all covered in dark grey smears on the front of our clothing and our bottoms. My hands were also covered in a grey powdery stain, and it seemed wherever we'd made direct contact with the steel girders we were covered in the same. We each saw this in turn and instinctively started brushing ourselves with our hands right in front of the cops. It was then quite obvious what we'd been doing. It must have been crystal clear to the cops too, but to their credit one of them simply said:

"Is anyone hurt?" to which he received no response. "Just as long as no-one's been hurt, okay?" he said, looking into the eyes of each of us in turn as we stood there looking and feeling like complete idiots.

"No, we're fine officer, thanks…" Dave replied, electing himself as group spokesperson. The cops looked around and before they could ask the obvious question Dave said: "My car's over there, we're just going home now…" There was a pause before one of the cops replied.

"Righto, make sure you do, and stay off the bridge okay?" and the two cops stood behind us on the bridge as our little grey-smeared band of reprobates made our way to Dave's car. The cops waited until we were all inside and driving away before they returned to their vehicle, thereby making sure we had actually gone. Just like the famous Harbour Bridge in Sydney, apparently you can now take official tours and organised climbs of the Story Bridge.

COORPAROO

Blood on the Rooftops

It became increasingly clear that Sean, Anika and Pat urgently needed an alternative source of revenue. We scanned the newspaper on the kitchen table one morning and found an ad for charity street collectors, collecting for the *Asthma Foundation of Queensland*. A percentage of what was taken in collection boxes was given to each collector, mainly for expenses rather than for an actual wage. It didn't require an interview or references of any kind so Sean, Pat, Anika and I set off the next day into the centre of Brisbane to the *Asthma Foundation* offices.

The person in charge at the *Asthma Foundation* was a quietly spoken middle-aged chap with a beard and initial impressions were that he seemed to be very pleasant and friendly. It was doubtful that he'd ever met anyone quite like our little group of miscreants before. After some brief introductions we were each given a brightly coloured vest to wear over our clothing, a charity collector's ID badge, and finally a wooden collecting box with a handle. There were some strict rules which applied to collecting. There was to be no coercion of the public or persistent shaking of the box in front of people, and the collecting was to be done in the precise areas as designated on the map. We all nodded in agreement and marched off out the door.

We had been told to go down to Brunswick Street in Fortitude Valley, which was in the city but some distance away from the main shopping and socialising areas. We tried it there for a while but we didn't have much success. Ignoring the rules completely we walked over to the Queen Street area and down the mall where our collecting boxes began to fill very quickly.

I was truly astonished at the generosity of some people, folding ten and even twenty dollar notes over and shoving them into my box. It grew very heavy with coins too, and we soon realised that standing by the side of the building line like a wallflower was not the best way to generate revenue.

Sean was by far the most outrageous. He ran up to people and directly invaded their personal space accosting them persistently like Michael Palin's lively ex-leper character street begging in *The Life of Brian* until they were forced to hand over money and put it in his collecting box. We had broken all the rules utterly, but within an hour every box was full to bursting and we had to return to the office.

Each collector could keep fifteen per cent of their takings. I had just over $100 in my first box and so I was given $16, and the others had taken virtually the same. We went back out straight away and returned after another hour, each with a similar amount again. The man in the office admitted he'd never seen anything like it and he probably suspected what was happening but why would he complain? He didn't ask any awkward questions but just kept taking the money. It is thanks to the creditable generosity of the people of Brisbane that we all filled four boxes that night and returned to Coorparoo with close to $50 each in our pockets. $20 went towards food and rent for the house, and the rest was sadly destined to be spent on booze.

We called in at a liquor store in Stones Corner on the way back to Coorparoo and returned to the house with twenty-four cans of Fosters. When these were consumed we staggered down to the nearest pub and blew the rest of our money on beer. At various times during that same evening Sean both ripped a deep cut in one hand that required stitches and also spent some time jumping around demonstrating Irish jigs on a wooden table in the pub. I'm not sure in what order these two events came about because it is all a bit of a hazy memory, but I know it was an absolutely mad night. Sean's finger spurted blood all over the place like a hosepipe and it was dressed by some medics in a very smart ambulance who to their credit wrote down that we were all 'No Fixed Abode'. They could tell what kind of people we were and if we'd been able to give an address which we initially tried to do, Sean would have had to pay something towards his treatment, which of course he couldn't.

We should have saved our money perhaps in order to find a place of our own so we didn't have to live like refugees on someone's floor, but we didn't. Collectively whenever we had money we spent it as soon as we had it. It sounds ridiculous that we had such little money and disposed of it so stupidly, but this behaviour is common amongst persons of lowly means. When you have nothing, and therefore have nothing to lose, life becomes something that exists purely for the moment, and nothing else really matters. Add to this the fact that life and your immediate prospects are probably so awful that whenever you can you will try to escape from it with booze or drugs. It's not in the least bit sensible, but there is a kind of twisted logic to it I suppose.

It was a Sunday night when Dave came around late and kept us all up smoking some very strong dope before he finally left at two o'clock. Sean and I then decided to go for a swim in the public pool. After climbing the fence we repeatedly threw ourselves into the water from the diving board both together in the dark doing impressions of the scene from *Butch Cassidy and the Sundance Kid* when the heroes jump off a cliff into a river far below. We were completely stoned off our heads and any such swimming in that condition was potentially very dangerous. Then there were lots of impressions of *E.T. The Extra Terrestrial*, which we'd recently seen, though the relevance to a diving board and a pool was lost somewhere, and finally some of the drowning scenes from *The Poseidon Adventure* were acted out on the pool steps under the water. There could quite easily have been some real life drowning that night, as we plunged to new depths of stupidity. We were eventually chased away by the resident pool attendant, and once back at the house I didn't get to sleep until four o'clock. I was up at eight o'clock that same morning for my job interview at the bank.

I was still buzzing when I woke up so I tried a cure for alcohol and THC intoxication which I made up on the spot: a huge mug of very strong black coffee with heaps of sugar and a large tablespoon of Vegemite, for the vitamin B. It tasted disgusting and probably did little to straighten me out. My eyes were still terribly bloodshot from both the cannabis and the chlorine in the pool, and I walked into the offices of the *ANZ Bank* on Queen Street in the city at nine twenty-five, with just five minutes to spare. I filled in a medical form and was directed along a corridor to wait outside a very plush office. Everywhere I looked there were shiny floors and acres of polished marble and it smelled strongly of cleaning fluid and money. I daydreamed about how wonderful it would be if I was given the job. I'd be able to get a cheap mortgage because I was working for a bank, and so I thought I might buy a small flat down at Kangaroo Point with a nice view of the city. I'd then get myself a cat, I'd frequently have friends around and I'd be a very sensible, sober, and upright citizen. It would be then, and only then, that I would contact Chrissie and ask her to come up from Sydney and stay with me for a while, maybe for several weeks at a time, lucky girl.

I was interviewed at length by two sharp-suited smiling gents who were very polite and courteous but there followed some deeply embarrassing moments when I realised that I didn't have an intelligent answer to quite a few of their questions. These were probably matters relating to banking, about which I really didn't know much or even care. Interviews are cleverly designed to weed out people who have this type of attitude. Very crafty. After half an hour of listening to myself mumble unintelligibly at my interviewers I was very gently advised to go home. I'd outwardly made more of an effort than at the bank in Darwin; I'd sent home for my suit which had arrived by parcel air freight a few days before, so at least I *looked* the part, not that it had done much good.

That afternoon I lay on the living room floor in my designated bed space, or at least the area of floor where I habitually slept like the family cat, and listened to music. It was stiflingly hot and there was no breeze of any sort. The humidity was higher than usual and it reminded me of Darwin. Just for a few minutes I longed for the touch of some freezing rain on my skin, some fog, and a cold, dismal English day. I put on an old tape of mine, *Wind and Wuthering* by Genesis, and the first line of the song *Blood on the Rooftops* bounced around inside my head.

Could it be that finally Australia, this wonderful sunburnt country, was losing its appeal? Quite often in life your subconscious will lead the way, like a big sister dragging you kicking and screaming to your first day at school. I started having vivid dreams of home and one morning I dreamt my parents were standing over me shaking me awake. It turned out to be Sean wanting to know if I had any cigarettes, but I found it curious that I was starting to think of home again. I'd been away from England for almost three years; maybe it was time to think about going back? I thought of my parents visiting Australia, but surely not in my present circumstances, while I was living like a hobo on someone's floor. If I had my own flat again like I had with Rich, then yes, everything would be fine. Again I imagined myself in a nice flat overlooking the city, where I would read or write in the evenings and not just sit and get pissed or stoned and gaze at the TV all the time. But who was this fantasy figure that didn't have any vices? Where on earth was he going to spring from? I was kidding myself.

As if by divine intervention the next day it rained like a monsoon in Brisbane. There were flash floods everywhere and the air filled with the sweet smell of wet roads and buildings long dried by many months of hot sun. All of us Europeans in the house ran outside laughing and shrieking with delight as we danced around in the warm rain, while the natives and the Kiwis just looked on bemused. Unlike British rain this was warm and pleasant to be in, and we allowed it to soak us through completely, it was so refreshing. A frequent change in the weather breaks the monotony and gives some punctuation to life. If the weather is identical every day for weeks or months it can bring a type of annoying boredom to it all, particularly if it is always uncomfortably hot. I remember Brendan, Steve and Gregg in Townsville telling me when I was there that the constant heat sometimes drove them a little bit mad. If one of them disappeared for a few hours in a temper the others would simply say "Oh it's okay, he's just gone a bit troppo..." and leave them to it.

As the Brisbane rains continued there were some spectacular displays of thunder and lightning with deep pools of rainwater filling the streets, reminiscent of the flooding in the Negev Desert, and it was all quite wonderful. It would cool the air very slightly for a while but then as the sun returned the lying moisture increased the humidity further, making the atmosphere even more oppressive.

Jane was successful in obtaining a job in a local elastic factory, with a regular wage and hours. She had entered Australia in the correct manner, with a work permit, and we were quite envious of her but pleased she was doing well. It seemed any job, however modest, was something valuable to cherish. It was a humbling experience having no money and living on the floor, but I was just beginning to have had quite enough of it.

Sean, Pat, Anika and I then tried our luck at strawberry picking. We travelled out towards the sea past Capalaba to Birkdale, where we stood bent over in an open field in sweltering heat like slaves for six hours from twelve noon until six o'clock for a measly $15.70. We had each managed to fill four large buckets of strawberries with just a cup of coffee for refreshment at half time. The bus fares alone reduced our money to such an extent that it was hardly worth doing. I returned to Coorparoo with a pounding headache that stayed with me for days. I became quiet and introspective as a result of the pain and made the following rather strange diary entry: '*I've had a feeling of utter exhaustion in me since as far back as childhood. As far as I can remember the best thing I can do is simply nothing at all...*'

That night someone produced some dope and passed a

bong around. My head was still pounding so I didn't have any. Later on for the first time I saw just how intoxicated and silly the others became and I wanted no more part of it. They say you can get a shock if you stay sober when all around you become intoxicated.

I needed to get away again. I was feeling too introspective and felt terribly trapped in the house at Coorparoo. It was an hour later when Dave turned up at the front door. He had a fortuitous business proposition for me, and it would mean moving out and living with him in another part of Brisbane.

FULL CIRCLE

"Got any room here for one more?"

Dave appeared at Brisbane magistrate's court the following day and was banned from driving having been caught several weeks before by the police for drunk-driving. I didn't even know he'd been caught. He therefore urgently needed someone to drive him around in his car, and he knew I was becoming unhappy at the Coorparoo house. I didn't even bother to barter for a better wage and accepted the first offer he made with free board and lodgings.

The next morning I took a bus into the city and then out to a house in Nicholson Street, Greenslopes. Dave's car was on the driveway, sitting there glinting in the sun, looking very shiny and powerful. Dave seemed delighted to see me and though it was never formally discussed, my presence was enough to acknowledge the fact that I'd accepted the job. We both sat on the front lawn with a coffee and a cigarette gazing across at the distant view of Brisbane city. It was calm and quiet, and I felt very relieved to be away from Coorparoo and living in some greater clarity. Fate has a way of dealing you an even hand of cards though, because later that day when we called by the house in Coorparoo I found a letter from the *ANZ Bank* informing me that I had been unsuccessful.

The house in Nicholson Street was a very tidy brick-built bungalow and was definitely a step up from Coorparoo. Dave was quite anxious the bedroom he had prepared for me didn't yet have a bed, but I stated I wasn't bothered. I'd lived for so long now on the floor that it wasn't a problem, and it really wasn't. I was just glad to have my own room and some peace, quiet, and solitude. I wrote for hours in my diary, and I wrote some poetry. I felt quite creative again.

I finally wrote a letter to Chrissie inviting her up to stay at the house in Greenslopes. At last I felt that I was able to show her that I had achieved something. Not only was I being paid $150 a week as a supervisor, but Dave was also paying me $80 a week to drive him around. I wasn't paying any tax and I didn't have any bills to pay. Things were certainly a little brighter and my letter to Chrissie was very persuasive. I was sure she would be on the next bus to Brisbane as soon as she read it.

After an absence of more than two weeks I saw Sean, Pat and Anika again. They called in to the office to meet up with one of the new lads called Steve. They were leaving Coorparoo, for whatever reason, and going to live with him in his tiny place in Highgate Hill, further into the city. It seemed they had no other option. The atmosphere between us was cool rather than frosty. I felt guilty for leaving them but thought I had no choice. It seemed they were considering making plans for a return to Europe.

On December 20th I received a disappointing postcard reply from Chrissie. She stated very briefly that she would not be coming up to Brisbane in the near future, though there was no real explanation. She also stated that she was moving to another part of Sydney and would send on her new address. For whatever reason this didn't arrive and it was then that contact was sadly lost. I never saw Chrissie again.

I began to save some real money for the first time since I'd arrived in Australia. My parents reminded me in their latest letter of some quite close relatives we had living in Auckland, New Zealand and they suggested I pay them a visit. They said they would write to them and ask them if it was possible. This set me thinking about my next move. I hadn't considered New Zealand before. Australia no longer seemed to be as attractive to me, despite the fact that I was now earning some fairly decent money. I felt as though something had died along the way and I was losing interest. The relationship I had with my friends Sean, Pat and Anika had broken up and Chrissie seemed lost to me. Was there anything else left? I considered that I'd seen as much of the country as I wanted to, so maybe it was time for me to move on.

Christmas arrived and I spent most of it at Dave's parents' place. It consisted of an entirely outdoor celebration with a barbeque party on the back lawn in sweltering, steamy midsummer heat. There were no real signs of Christmas anywhere, unlike in Europe. Dave's parents had a small Christmas tree on a table but it seemed little more than a token gesture. Christian countries across the northern hemisphere made Christmas a huge event, lighting up their streets and houses for weeks, thereby bringing some brightness and cheer to the deepest and darkest part of winter. It really did seem particularly odd to be enduring such heat and bright light at Christmas time. I'd spent winters in the Middle East before, but even there it was quite cool and dark in December.

New Year celebrations in Brisbane passed in a predictable haze of champagne and cannabis, mainly at Dave's place. His sister Eileen was staying and so were some of the people who were working in the company. I'd had a brief relationship of sorts with Eileen and even though it didn't last there was no animosity between us. There was a good atmosphere and the New Year was seen in very well. We watched from the front lawn at midnight as we could see fireworks exploding high over the city during a particularly warm New Year's Eve. I thought it was actually quite brilliant to see in the New Year in shorts and a t-shirt, instead of standing around in some very cold and damp public place shivering half to death. Clearly Australia still had its merits.

The weeks passed and the anniversary approached of my arrival in Australia. I reflected on my time there and the greatest episode was surely my hitchhiking expedition around the country. I could hardly believe I'd done it myself, and I wrote about it frequently in my diary, jotting down various incidents in greater detail to keep for posterity, and ultimately for this book. I mooted the possibility to Dave that I was considering moving on, flying across to New Zealand to stay with relatives. I rang my parents for the first time in months and my mother informed me that my cousin would apparently be delighted to put me up for a while in Auckland. The idea became an increasingly attractive one. She also informed me that my sister Sally had recently found out she was pregnant with twins. Finally my mother said a curious thing to me about my travels which she later repeated: "To what end, all this anxiety?"

Dave's attitude to me changed noticeably when it was clear that I was increasingly serious about leaving Australia. Our relationship became cooler and more business-like, and the joy-rides around the city together while listening to Jean-Michel Jarre became far less frequent. Our conversations and games of backgammon also suffered, dwindling to virtually nothing. It is a strange game to be played when a relationship cools. Instead of trusting and accepting all the quick jumps across the board they are observed closely and counted with suspicion which then slows the game and it loses much of its spontaneity as a result.

The end came several weeks into the New Year when I accidentally reversed Dave's car into a wooden post at the end of the driveway in Nicholson Street. The rear offside was quite badly dented, and the boot would no longer close. It was the end of the week and I was due to collect my wages, plus some money owed from the previous week. I needed the money for my forthcoming trip to New Zealand, though nothing had been formally arranged yet. It was also the last week that I had to drive for Dave, as his relatively brief driving ban was over and he had just been given his driving licence back.

"It must be good to be driving again, eh?" I said to Dave as I sat down in the office.

"Yeah, it is," Dave said, looking distracted and preoccupied while dropping some papers in a desk drawer. There was a long silence and then Dave looked at me with a very serious expression firmly fixed across his face. "I'm not going to pay you, Jonathan."

"What? Why not? What do you mean?" I replied as I tried to force a smile, hoping this was a joke.

"There's more damage to the car than I first thought, take

a look at it. You must have hit the boot fast, it was open wasn't it?"

"Well, yes, I suppose...but you're insured aren't you?"

"I have to pay the first five hundred bucks, and I'm going to need that..."

So he was going to keep the $500 he owed me in order to pay the insurance excess, leaving me desperately short of money. I couldn't believe what I was hearing. How could he do that to me? Dave just sat staring at me in his high-backed brown leather office chair with practiced fake sincerity on his face. The next moment Dave opened a drawer and said:

"Do you wanna smoke?"

I stood up to leave. I couldn't stay with this person a moment longer. I felt betrayed and abandoned. Clearly to him I'd been an employee all along, and not the friend that I thought I was.

"No I don't," I replied, "I need to concentrate. I need to find some money from somewhere," I said to Dave as I walked out of the office for the last time. Dave shouted after me:

"See you later!" to which I didn't even turn around but just replied:

"Yeah..." and walked out. I never saw Dave again.

I couldn't stay at Dave's place any longer. But where could I go? I returned to the house at Nicholson Street and packed my little rucksack with my meagre possessions and locked the door. I posted the key through the letter box and walked away. I knew of Steve's address in Highgate Hill where Sean, Pat and Anika were staying. Could I contemplate living there? Were they even still in the country? I had shamefully lost contact and now I needed them I wanted their friendship again. I certainly wouldn't think of returning to Coorparoo to the Kiwis, if they were even still there. I had more in common with the Europeans, and they were after all the better friends.

I felt like the Prodigal Son knocking on Steve's door. I was nervous and felt ashamed. How would they react to me returning to them? Pat answered the door and invited me in immediately, without hesitation.

"Come on in, man, how've you been, not seen you for a while." Pat was a lovely unassuming Irishman who saw the good in everyone. Sean and Anika were in the kitchen preparing some food.

"Got any room here for one more?" I said, standing in the kitchen doorway, probably sounding quite desperate. I felt incredibly remorseful as though I would burst into tears at any moment.

"Jonathan, you're back? What happened to Dave?" Sean said, looking behind me in case Dave suddenly appeared.

"I've finished up there. I need somewhere to live…"

I explained what had happened and they didn't seem at all surprised. They told me of their own disasters too. For a few weeks they'd lived with some of Pat's relatives in Sydney before they threw the three of them out for being 'un-Australian' by not being more active in seeking employment. Hence the move in with Steve to their current two-room ground floor tenement. This was after the Kiwis had thrown them out of Main Avenue, Coorparoo. It seemed that once I'd left they felt no loyalty to the three of them and they simply told them to leave. It's a cutthroat world out there.

At Highgate Hill all the neighbours were foreigners who didn't speak any English, and there were apparently as many wild children running around as wild animals and insects. There was a wide selection of Australian wildlife in the place, with several different types of quite vicious ants and some enormous and very numerous cockroaches living in every room of the building. How can an ant being so tiny have the courage to pick a fight and start nipping a human being, a creature ten thousand times their size? The cockroaches were not too bothered either, and for me it was Warners Avenue all over again. At least there were no Scientologists running around, no strange women getting bombed off their tits while knitting, and no randy young women wanting me to shag them, though the latter would have been quite nice at the time.

What we did have was a rather strange chap called Jeff, who

was apparently one of Steve's mates. He was a little younger than us and an Aussie like Steve. He told us repeatedly that he'd lived for a while up the coast in Gladstone, and whenever he spoke he seemed to prefix his conversations with the line: "When I was in Gladstone..." He did nothing all day, every day, and when he collected his dole money he would just spend it all on huge tubs of ice cream which he would sit down and eat in front of us, without offering any of it to anyone.

All food had to be wrapped up tight or kept in the fridge or it would just be heaving with insects in no time. Not that we ever seemed to have much food. In fact Sean recently reminded me that we used to keep melon skins, that is just the skins with nothing attached to them, in the empty fridge so that at least it would *appear* to have something in it. I thought of the irony in the fact that very soon I would be leaving Australia and I was in the exact same position as I had been just after my arrival a year before. My fortunes had turned full circle.

I rang home, reversing the charges. New Zealand was all arranged. I bought a single ticket to Auckland with *Air New Zealand* for $266, the cheapest I could find. Luckily I wasn't asked for a visa and I didn't have one. I only just had enough money, as usual. My flight was set for the following Saturday at twelve-thirty, just after midday. My relatives would collect me from Auckland airport at six forty-five local time. So that was it, I was finally leaving Australia after almost exactly twelve months.

My last few days in Oz were inevitably a crazy time. Gareth and his friend Ronald would call around regularly and bring with them beer, wine and cannabis. My last week is a very hazy memory and my diary entries were haphazard, but a lot happier than they had been. Sean, Anika and Pat were also arranging their departure but had nothing fixed by the time I left.

On the morning of my last day we all piled into Gareth's parents four-by-four and drove to the airport. We sat near Departures in the car park smoking dope until we ran out. I was completely off my face for the last time in Australia. It was incredibly hot at thirty-five degrees Celsius and the air was heavy and sticky with the humidity. I said my goodbyes with a few tears and left my little tent with Sean and Anika before making my way into the airport building.

When the Australian Immigration officers saw my passport, two smartly dressed men in suits took me to one side and then into an interview room. My six week tourist visa had expired ten and a half months before. "Where have you stayed? What have you been doing? How have you supported yourself?" were the questions fired at me amongst many others. My eyes were redder than Dracula's after all the smoking in the car and I knew I must have looked intoxicated from something. I just replied with vague statements about being supported from home and living with friends. Eventually after about twenty minutes – which seemed like hours to me – they stamped my passport with something quite large and let me go. I was leaving the country anyway, so what more could they do?

I stepped inside the *Air New Zealand* aircraft with nineteen dollars in my pocket. As it thundered down the runway and smoothly lifted off Australian soil I felt relieved to be leaving. There was a lively buzz in the aircraft because New Zealand was thrashing Australia at cricket, and as a gorgeous stewardess handed me a complimentary whiskey I tried to list the highlights of my astonishing twelve month stay. Was it seeing Sydney Harbour and the opera house close up for the first time? Could it have been the midnight ride in the back of the Ute while crossing central Queensland dodging the sleeping animals? What about the drive with Rod and Ritchie, or passing through the spectacular emptiness of *The Red Centre* around Alice Springs, or even when I saw Chrissie again in Adelaide?

I had learned some harsh lessons while in Oz, and some of them would stay with me forever. Even when enduring great hardship you can make the best of things, be happy and enjoy life, because you don't always need pots of money, just enough will suffice. Looking out the window I saw the New South Wales coastline disappear behind the aircraft. I raised my little plastic glass and the ice cubes chinked very gently as I said a final farewell toast to Australia. It was all over.

POETRY

I wrote quite a lot of poetry when I was in Australia, and much of it has been lost. I dare to think that some of it is reasonably good and was written when in quiet contemplative moments, but a lot of it was composed when I'd either been smoking dope or drinking booze, or both. If you don't like poetry then perhaps the following wouldn't be of interest, but these fifteen poems form part of the story and I've included them all, good and bad, and in the correct chronological order.

Sydney

Sydney

Sex without love but at the moment
Death with Allen's phrases when second,
But even she doesn't know to be wrapped,
I didn't on Wednesday and again,
But the night, all night, happen between Phil,
Wrapped to one and all,
Going to see what happens,
Plenty of jam jars for you, baby.

How old are you, thirty-two?
A trip to Denver for five others,
Get wanderers for your trousers
I've been cut off! It's an emergency!
Applause! You've won the prize!
Thank you for a wonderful year,
Come in, all the best from me to you,
Your arms, hunchback.

The wind howls on the Weekend Special,
A few showers over Australia's number one city
Now showing at the city opera house
A brand new kitchen
We do more for you personally
A taste of summer
Sequences where the colours changed
This mad film.

It was all very impulsive
Therefore suffered the consequences
Celebrate the fact that you are alive
We don't know who you are
How much love can we give?
Sgt Pepper?

Bondi

Vander mint is an excellent booze and shaving plant,
Flowers in my eyes and bricks in my vase,
Books up my hole and he's drunk,
No, really pissed, eh?
Got to listen to the sunrise,
Never hear Robert any more,
Only in commercials
Michelle,
But I don't even have a bike,
No-one's coming here to see my garage collection,
And the radio's new batteries I bought
Next week as I travelled the fourth dimension,
That of Bondi shopping precinct
Where stamps are five thousand miles wide
And people talk about the end of worm's influence
On JF Kennedy's wife's poodle's lamppost
Urinating areas of Washington DC,
Or even how certain women in your life
You can never forget
And the price of Rice Crispies
Of frog's legs in the Gambia
Where dark people get the best melons
With suntans and monkeys work as brickies
And giraffes as dandelions
That make burdock for the disc jockeys
To drink and eat and sleep
On hundreds of bottles of Ludwig pianos
And Tia Maria and Coca-Cola.
Gary has seen the light.

Warners Avenue

All work and no play makes Jack a dull boy
All play and no work makes Jack a poor boy,
All, none, nil, nothing, no, never, not gone,
Gone, piss off, fuck off, naff off, leave off, go
Go zoom, sex, lust, tits, cunts, boobs, thighs, tits,
Cars, vans, helicopters, ships, planes, flowers
Marijuana, hashish, cocaine, lysergide, pounds,
Shillings, fast lane, lane lament, incorporate
Empathy, sympathy, dextrosol, dexterity, energy
Radio, Germany, hate hate, kill kill,
Kill, bomb, gas, shoot, destroy, *Destry Rides Again*,
Down, down, further insane, loopy, mad, cracked,
Warners Avenue, money money, thirty five death,
Lust, love, must love, love you, pain, pain,
Pain, heartache, death, saucers, cups, spoons
Ash, cigarettes, filters, chips, love, fish fish,
Kashmir, McDonald's, no no not again, look, see,
Hear, feel, listen, kill kill, Miss Miss, miss you,
Pain, sun, steps, laugh laugh, cry, cry, radio, goodbye.

Brisbane

Maps

Death lurking around each telegraph pole
A lust for a word, crying to be free,
Sitting and lying then standing talking
The music is the trickery, staring,
Eyes straining but seeing nothing,
White walls, ghosts, ghouls, and stereo noise
Sydney, Canberra and printing maps
Coloured wires, church congregations
Drum kits filling my garage, rolling down my steps,
Beach faces, hips, thighs, smiles,
Sunshine and heavy rain, autumn friends
Yellow wardrobe, earthy water, twelve to two
Drum, Israel, past and darkness,
Under the sheets, Beatles and my jumper,
Stamps and beauty, never lose your eyes my friend,
Never leap into the handle's movement,
Don't open the door, Jimmy,
Kill your stainless, your green and yellow and black,
I won't, but maybe I will, but I might not,
May never ever be coming back.

You

Run and hide behind my tape,
Keep your legs for me,
Stay away from smoke, but drive away free,
I cannot see you but I know your cigarettes
I taste you in my brain
Your bits of spew, everything in the drawer,
But who's the bed head now?
Round you tick like time to reflect,
Emotions murdering, freaking me out,
You rip my box so I lose my cans
My jeans are disturbed, a crinkled mess,
Touch me again and I think I'll cry
But I'll reverberate and challenge, maybe die,
Dance and fry your own eggs,
He leaves again and knows you too,
I care and I hate, I love and celebrate,
Leave off my cells, stranger,
You're killing my desires
My feet dangle over the end of the bed.

Loss

Exit my soul and run through my trees
Find the path on your own
Orientate your own wardrobe
Hang your own virgin habitational dreams
Leave me out of your sunny autumn
And your golden view is a sewer
Your stereo a horror movie special effect
I hate your table, burn my chairs,
Seconds and premonitions, horror and pain,
I never sat there and never touched you,
Cleaning and hanging your blinds
That blotted me out of your life
Hosing down my fire and killing
Peter, Paul, Mary and Morrison,
Hair and beard, vanity and grace
Bedspreads is all I think of,
And Rod Stewart and Debbie Harry
Brisbane, Queensland, the Premier choice,
I was given no choice at all.

The flat

Babies are crying to their own sounds
No-one cares except God,
And he's gone out, not home today
Who do you turn to when all the rhythm's gone?
What happens when the light is over?
How can we laugh in the dark?
Get up and not say hello?
Rain on our thoughts in colour and stereo
Strength trembling and fear growing
Curtains closed but blinds half open
No sounds outside but the din of night
No whiskey, no drugs, no celestial sight,
Even the stars have run away.

Sick

We all look sick
But I cannot change time
And nothing goes well
The memories flood my hair,
Reluctant *Human League* player
Hidden meanings in everything I see
Sniff your mind away
Down the avenue of trees and dollars
And no-one will laugh
As you cry and slowly die and rot
You'll go septic and sour
We'll all get worse by the hour
Yellow will be the colour of the future
Everything tumbling and nothing working
The Earth on the dole, the System gone
All bags will be packed
All pasts will be futures
Regrets become agonies
And longings of experience
Life gone
All is too late.

God, love, Scotch

God is love
But who and where is God?
It stands therefore,
That 'Where is love?'
God is omnipresent
Love is the same
But where?
How long is a piece of string?
God knows
But where is the answer?
It must be here
In me, myself, I
I am the answer, no:
Scotch solves ALL!

Home

No, not any more,
I'm sorry, but that's a lie
I'm not sorry, I'm only happy when I'm miserable
I'm sick, tired, and depressed,
I wish it was Christmas
I miss Christmas
Christmas at home
Or on Be'eri
The tree
All the lights
Walking on snow
Throwing snowballs
Driving in the sleet and slush
Racing like hare and hounds
To the guys and girls
Only to think it a waste
So where do I go?
I need.

Clarity

I took you all along
And gave you all I could
The truth in me was better
The night for me was settled
Yet I walked with empty pockets
And an obliging, working spirit;
What do you mean 'Sorry?'
I have no key to the 27th floor
So what's in it, being sorry or glad?
To trudge through the lonely transparency of life
I opened all the doors and was alone,
I lost; I got out, never tasting champagne
But occasional nurses were good neighbours
As I danced and sighed, lazily,
Sipping the soft taste of money
Angry and confused I crumble away
Raising to the toast of light and music
Auld Lang Syne old friends apart,
Crazy ways, crazy life, crazy end,
Run as fast as possible up the stairs,
To horror and death,
No, to life and love.

Confusion

Range my city views from the penthouse
Listen now of a time long past,
Smash to bits the steel building veranda
Give me back my legal process
Before Christmas to hide under the presents
Relative to the bird of prey of my mind
And never give up on me
Never ever take from me to kill my soul
You would sacrifice The Clash in my head
Approach the cold you would find
The snow and closed senior windows
Draw my support from Britain
A far off Kalashnikov chatters
The threat to the world
The world threatens itself
The ferocious idea for a wonderful
Spaced out Greek and Italian
Consume paint, build and eat,
All to the phone
Walt Disney never said it
Think opposite
Never trust your primary emotions
Nor feel your fear, or fear your feelings
A juicy woman and a filled stomach
Peace of mind and piece of cake
Rosy performances and fields of oaks,
Following the beautiful sky
Across the page of your life
Write your own life as best you can
Let not others either dictate nor stumble
Follow what is written in your book.

Bonjour! (With apologies to French speakers)

Ne dit pas l'horreur "au revoir!"
Quand ou est la vie?
Et où est le soleille brille,
Mon crème et frises?
Pas d'été
Maintenant, j'habite
En hiver
Donnez-moi une autre chance
Pour une autre après-midi
Au bord de la rivière solaire
Quel temps avez-vous
Avec ces jours malades?

Stoned again

The truth shall follow on like man after woman
Like music to your ears filled with life and movement
Never cease by comparison, give points and credit
To those of feeble language, they kill people like us
Save all you can, as possessions are transcendental
To the spirit, building blocks of the soul
Your fixation to your origin on the planet
Where body and soul rejoice in needlessness
Beware twisted images, repulses of sight
But never shy away, as life is as broad as
The universe and we are but our own religion
And never get stoned on good marijuana
On an empty bloody stomach –
See you next episode!

Seasons

I long for the shadow of a cold green field,
The chill bite of a northerly wind
Cold toes, cold nose, and paralysed cold fingers
Hatred reversed, I long for love of hates
A relief from love, sight and sound released
Oh this chill air, moist with my confusion
The sun is forever with us here, he never rests,
But at night, then he's left his mark on the land,
His soul warming us even in the darkness
Where are those crisp, obscured days of my past?
Those fire-lit, sheltered, calm evenings?
The so old mist-enshrouded oaks, waiting for us
To walk among them, helping us to pass the cold,
All life, all concentration to pass the frost,
A love so strong as never seen here
As all of us love to be warm, so warm
We try to shut out the cold
Yet it brings with it so much beauty
Running and returning to and fro
What life in constant heat
Can bring the desire, strong enough to make meet
The future days of eternal life?
With renewed springtime vigour
We scowl in the sun; our sight will miss the figure
The one we'll never know
I know I miss the warmth of the snow
Scotch and the firelight glow
Yes, eventually, to England I must go.

ACKNOWLEDGEMENTS

I have to thank Australia for being there and changing me the way it did. It is a truly wonderful country. I've revisited several times since I left, and it still holds a special place in my heart. I'd like to thank Jeremy Thompson and his team at Matador, including the copy editor and proof reader and everyone involved in the process of turning these sun-bleached scribbled notes into something vaguely worth reading.

My thanks to Sean, Pat, Anika and Jane for variously helping me out when I was in Australia and Sean in particular for recently helping me to remember some of the events. Thanks to curtisbrown.com.au for the use of the second verse of the wonderful Dorothea Mackellar poem 'My Country'. By arrangement with the Licensor, the Dorothea Mackeller Estate, c/- Curtis Brown (Aust) Pty Ltd.

I'd like to thank the people who printed the brilliantly detailed map of Australia which I cut up so shamelessly for my diary and then inserted into this book. Whoever you are, thank you! I'd like to thank anyone else involved in my story for their contribution to it all.

Finally, if you haven't yet visited Australia, then what on earth are you waiting for?

Jonathan Nicholas
March 2014